THE FISHERMAN AND THE RHINOCEROS

Eric Briys is a managing director at Deutsche Bank where he heads the Insurance Strategies Group. He has worked previously for Merrill Lynch and Lehman Brothers. Prior to joining the investment banking world he was a Professor of Finance at the HEC School of Management. He has published six books on finance and economics and more than thirty scientific articles.

François de Varenne is a vice-president at Deutsche Bank where he covers European insurance and reinsurance companies. He has worked previously for Merrill Lynch and Lehman Brothers. Prior to joining the investment banking world he was Head of financial and economics affairs at the French Federation of Insurance Companies. An engineer, an actuary and a PhD in finance by training he has published two books and more than ten scientific articles.

THE FISHERMAN AND THE RHINOCEROS

Eric Briys and François de Varenne

JOHN WILEY & SONS, LTD

Chichester · New York · Weinheim · Brisbane · Singapore · Toronto

Originally published in French under the title *La mondialisation financiere:
Enfer ou Paradis?* © 1999, Economica, 2-7178-3701-9

Other Wiley Editorial Offices

John Wiley & Sons, Inc., 605 Third Avenue,
New York, NY 10158-0012, USA

Wiley-VCH Verlag GmbH, Pappelallee 3,
D-69469 Weinheim, Germany

Jacaranda Wiley Ltd, 33 Park Road, Milton,
Queensland 4064, Australia

John Wiley & Sons (Asia) Pte Ltd, 2 Clementi Loop #02-01,
Jin Xing Distripark, Singapore 129809

John Wiley & Sons (Canada) Ltd, 22 Worcester Road,
Rexdale, Ontario M9W 1L1, Canada

British Library Cataloguing in Publication Data

A catalogue record for this book is available from the British Library

ISBN 0-471-88961-X

Typeset in Goudy by Footnote Graphics, Warminster, Wiltshire
Printed and bound in Great Britain by Antony Rowe Ltd, Chippenham, Wiltshire

This book is printed on acid-free paper responsibly manufactured from sustainable
forestation, for which at least two trees are planted for each one used for paper
production.

To Aurore, Flora, Marie, Jean and Clement

To Marie-Laure and Capucine

'The happy man is one whose activity accords with perfect virtue and who is adequately furnished with external goods'

Aristotle

'Wall Street strives to take the mystery out of tomorrow'

Merryle Stanley Rukeyser

CONTENTS

INTRODUCTION

Economics is not the same thing as politics; it is not concerned in any way with either the distribution or the balance of power; but it allows us to understand how nations procure what they need for their subsistence. Now, since these things are due to the efforts of private individuals, and since they are mostly owned by private individuals, a nation's economy cannot be regarded as being exclusively the business of politicians: it is everybody's business. However, one cannot expect every citizen to be well versed in this science. Everyone cannot know everything; but it is very possible and very desirable that as a rule people should not have misconceptions about anything, especially about those things that it is in their interest to understand.

This vigorous foreword opens the 'Catéchisme d'économie politique' written by Jean-Baptiste Say (1821), a brilliant nineteenth-century French economist. Say decided in 1821 to produce what he called his 'catechism', namely an informal guide, designed to 'explain in everyday language the main facts of economics'. His aim was to write an educational piece. Indeed, he refused to believe that economics was the exclusive playground of experts. He viewed economics as part of everyone's daily life. The main ambition of his 'catechism' was to explain to his contemporaries 'how wealth is produced, distributed and consumed in society'. However, he was aware that this was not an easy task. Writing a technical book for a restricted audience of experts is often easier than writing a simple, instructive text for a large set of layreaders. Say firmly emphasised the need 'to be clear, without going into all the details, examples and proofs which present each object in all its aspects and in every light'. In such a venture images and metaphors are a welcome vehicle for exploration.

The present book is very much in this tradition. It aims to be a companion guide to the intricate world of modern international finance. This seemingly mysterious world is too often accused of causing the many plagues that affect our economies, such as job losses, corporate restructurings, economic disruptions. In that sense, international finance is no different from economics. As early as 1946, Henry Hazlitt was upset by the fact that 'economics is haunted by more fallacies than any other study known to man'. He viewed this rather unfortunate state of affairs as 'the persistent tendency of men to see only the immediate effects of a given policy, or its effects only on a special group, and to neglect to inquire what the long-run effects of that policy will be not only on that special group but on all groups'.

Again, international finance is no exception. However, it has now a new companion in crime and that companion is generally known today as 'globalisation'. This new partnership has instigated the creation of new fallacies, such as the supposedly demonic trend of financial speculation and its destabilising effects. Unfortunately, these fallacies seem to have the ability to spread out more rapidly than the financial globalisation that they try to censure!

Times change, and so do economic systems. Economic affairs, without a doubt, affect us even more closely than they did Say and his contemporaries. The ubiquity of capital flows, free trade, unemployment, the fall of the Berlin Wall, the Asian and Russian upheavals and the soaring stock exchanges are among the many phenomena which witness how sensitive to economic changes societies all over the world have become. The market economy is surging forward everywhere. Some people regard this as an inevitable trend and they applaud the fact that the 'invisible hand' of Adam Smith (1776) is strengthening its grip. Smith, a strong advocate of free markets, firmly believed that the individual is 'led by an invisible hand to promote an end which was not part of his intention'. Smith was convinced that, by pursuing his own interest, the individual 'frequently promotes that of the society more effectually than when he really intends to promote it'. For others, the rise of the global market economy is a diabolical mechanism, which 'can destabilize what might have seemed rock-solid economies – as happened in Asia' (Giddens, 1999). It entails money being placed above everything, or the domination of the weak by the strong. The misgivings do not stop there. The French economist Henri Bourguinat (1995) goes one step further and speaks of the tyranny of the markets. In his opinion, the most revealing evidence of this tyranny is the impressive growth of financial markets, and more specifically of the so-called derivatives market encompassing complex financial devices such as options, futures, swaps and hybrids. Anthony Giddens, Director of the London School of Economics, notes that the daily volume transacted on the foreign exchange markets is, measured as a stack of hundred-dollar notes, twenty times higher than Mount Everest. As a matter of fact, hardly a day passes without the press getting agitated about the astounding pace of development of the financial markets. This fast pace is usually castigated with reference to the various scandals and casualties that these markets are said to engender. Barings, Lloyd's of London, Herstatt, Metallgesellschaft, Crédit Lyonnais, American Savings and Loans, Procter & Gamble, Orange County, Long Term Capital Management – there is apparently no shortage of spectacular collapses or near-collapses.

The basic question, though, is simple. Is the globalisation of finance steering us towards heaven or hell? Ought we to be afraid of the new economic system that we live in? Should we fear the financial markets and their infamous derivatives? Should we be dreading the prospect of a domino effect that will drag the world economy into a chain of one collapse after another? In short, have we, like Frankenstein, given birth to creatures which can no longer be controlled and which are a permanent threat to our future?

These questions are far-reaching enough to warrant an in-depth treatment. Too often, as Hazlitt reminded us, today's economic systems and financial markets are thought of in terms more appropriate to the script of a psychological drama. This is the sure recipe to obfuscation and misunderstanding. Instead, a common-sense method of explaining and understanding what goes on in these markets is required. This, at any rate, is the task of the present book. This is also the reason for its peculiar structure.

Three parables are narrated. The first parable brings together a fisherman and a rhinoceros. This rather surprising duo is predicated on a recommendation formulated by the nineteenth-century French economist Frédéric Bastiat (1850) who insisted on the distinction to be drawn between 'what is seen and what is unseen'. Indeed, many economic observers tend to present attractive arguments but overlook the main issues. For instance, they express deep concerns and denounce the ascendancy ('what is seen') of the financial economy over the so-called real economy. The image of an over-inflated financial bubble threatening to burst at any moment is recurrent in their commentaries. This gloom-mongering is at the very least questionable. In economics, as well as in biology, there is still no evidence at all for spontaneous generation. The first parable teaches that the expansion of the financial economy is rather a mere reflection of the tyranny of the real economy ('what is unseen or on purpose unseen'). Indeed, the tyranny of the real economy causes a lot of harm in many different places. It hampers the freedom of action of economic agents. It forces them to cope with risks that jeopardise the well-deserved rewards of their daily labour. The rhinoceros and the fisherman show how this freedom can be regained by resorting to the vast panoply of solutions offered by international finance.

The characters in the second parable are a blind pearl-fisher and the legendary Apache chief Geronimo. This pair, just as odd as the first, begs a key question: How much confidence can individuals or firms place in the financial institutions managing their savings? Geronimo learnt the tough way how often trust can be betrayed. To rare exceptions, the word of US Cavalry officers was certainly not their bond. Savers worldwide have learnt a similar painful and costly lesson. Financial institutions are not bullet proof and some may even go bankrupt. Savings of a lifetime can be wiped out because they have been invested either with a lame duck institution or a gambling bank. These events, when they occur, are quickly used as another example of the failed promises that proliferate in the modern financial economy.

Unfortunately, these hasty interpretations are too often drawn from a scapegoat type of argument. In a nutshell, financial instruments, chief among them derivatives, are said to be toxic. They represent some sort of wild beast that has escaped from its cage and is roaming the countryside of the real economy causing indiscriminate damage. Hence, the collapse of an old UK banking institution, Barings, was blamed on the derivatives market and another entry was made on the debit side by those seeking to prosecute the wild animal. The shock caused by the downfall of a jewel of the British establishment was indeed enormous. However, a more cautious analysis and a revisit of Barings history would have helped in avoiding misleading judgments. Indeed, it is ironic that Barings had already experienced collapse or near-collapse on several occasions in the past. Fernand Braudel (1979), the French historian of capitalism, tells the story of one of these near-bankruptcies. It was the expensive outcome of a risky speculation in cochineal. Cochineal, the scarlet colouring used for textile and food dyes, is obtained from a Mexican insect. As Braudel points out, it is a luxury product that has good preservative qualities. In 1787, Barings, in partnership with a financier called Henry Hope, decided to gain control of the stocks of cochineal throughout Europe, in expectation of a rather poor harvest. They bought up stocks in Marseilles, Rouen, Hamburg and St Petersburg, hoping to take advantage of the price rise triggered by their manipulation of the cochineal market. However, they had not factored the sudden war between Turkey and Russia and the crisis in the French textile industry into their speculative equation. As a result, demand for cochineal dropped. Prices fell and the venture came to an abrupt end. In no-one's book could the structure and power of the financial economy be blamed for this disaster! Yet, two centuries later, the Kobe earthquake took Nick

Leeson's speculative gamble by surprise and foiled an equally risky undertaking! Leeson's speculative move blew up and killed Barings. But, this time the pariah of the financial markets was deemed to be at the root of the problem. Barings is also part of nineteenth-century literature. Indeed, on a more anecdotal note, Phileas Fogg, the main character of *Around the World in Eighty Days* (Jules Verne, 1873) had to find a bank to sponsor his famous venture. Interestingly enough, Jules Verne picked Barings! Some things do not seem to change!

The third parable put a thirteenth-century Genoese merchant and some molecules together. This parable focuses on the management of risks that plague our daily actions. For instance, inflation may bite into our future pensions, bad weather may destroy a farmer's crop, adverse foreign currency movements may bankrupt an otherwise flourishing business. A passive stance *vis-à-vis* these risks can be short-sighted and ultimately hazardous. The parable prompts us to carefully consider the goals of active risk management and the means used to achieve proper risk redistribution. Banks and insurance companies are familiar institutions with whom we place some of our risks. We invariably take their existence for granted. We regard them as being institutions that are 'genetically speaking' very different from each other, fulfilling clearly distinct functions. Banks manage our savings and lend us money. Insurance companies insure us against damage caused by fire, theft, floods, etc.... But, if we look at banks and insurance companies more closely – that is, through the eyes of a thirteenth-century Genoese merchant – it becomes less certain that our perception of these institutions is the right one. It is even more doubtful whether it throws any light at all on the future.

The Genoese merchant, Benedetto Zaccaria, teaches us that what matters most is the function that needs to be fulfilled, rather than the institution delivering it. The Genoese merchant wants to protect his business from any misfortune that unpredictable sea-storms or the menacing skull and crossbones might have in store for him. It is of the utmost importance to him to be able to transfer these risks. In other words, he needs to secure an insurance cover against the hostility of either Mother Nature or the pirates. It seems quite obvious that this is the corporate mandate of insurance companies. However, the solution he chose, in 1298, turns out to be a hybrid one. An insurer, a speculator or a bank could provide it equally. What matters is that Benedetto Zaccaria, a successful Genoese merchant, can reap the dividends of his business talent without having to fear any misfortune caused by events over which he has no control.

In this respect, it is rather fortunate that there is such a vast array of solutions available to remove unwanted risks: banks, insurance companies, financial markets, etc. Even more fortunate is the fact that the new finance – 'cyber-finance or e-finance', as some might call it – has engineered various new instruments that work, where the traditional ones have failed. The parable teaches us that there is no divorce between the real economy and the financial economy. On the contrary, the international financial economy is useful because it removes the viscosity of the real economy. It puts the economic agents in a position of responsibility by ensuring that they have the opportunity to accept only those risks they are able to manage through the exercise of their own particular skills. It also provides some litmus test whereby economic agents can prove that they have valuable skills for society as a whole. Indeed, skills or the absence thereof are easier to decipher once parasitic risks have been eradicated. Benedetto Zaccaria transported and sold alum. Once the perils of the sea had been removed from his business through a clever transaction, he was able to show that his activity was indeed useful and profitable. The same holds true for the banker and the insurer who have to demonstrate their usefulness and their legitimacy to their clients.

This is not always easy. Thus, in the United States, the traditional banks have been steadily pushed out of the mortgage market, of which they now have only a small share. Financial market and investment banks have taken over. Mortgages have become negotiable and are now traded on a very active market. In other words, property finance has taken a different direction from the one we have been familiar with so far. We can borrow more easily from banks because banks are no longer limited by the size of their own balance sheets. Their constraints are no longer our constraints.

The use of parables might seem rather 'Biblical' to some. Detours and digressions are worthwhile. The shortest route is not always a straight line, especially when it comes to dismantling economic and financial fallacies. To understand and to explain both requires patience and acumen. Thus, when Robert Louis Stevenson decided in 1878 to explore the French Cévennes, he chose a rather surprising means of transportation: a little donkey that he named Modestine (1878). For a Scotsman, laden as he was with gear, this was certainly a risky choice. In the late nineteenth century, the Gévaudan Mountains[1] were daunting, cold and deserted. Nevertheless, what a clever choice

---

[1] The Gévaudan Mountains are famous for the mysterious beast that devoured women, children and cattle from spring 1764 to June 1767.

it was on his part. Like all donkeys, Modestine is full of wisdom and blessed with a special talent for long-distance trekking. She cultivates the art of curiosity, of geography and of making detours. We are particularly fond of Modestine. The following parables owe much to her approach.

THE PARABLE OF THE FISHERMAN
AND THE RHINOCEROS

What is the difference between a rhinoceros in Zambia and a fisherman off the UK coast of Cornwall or the French coast of Brittany? Short question, short answer: the former will survive, the latter may not! This is a bitter and surprising paradox. Every day environmentalists raise the alarm, warning us about the seemingly programmed destruction of our planet. Endangered species, the greenhouse effect, holes in the ozone layer, pollution, environmental damage are familiar as well as disquieting notions.

However, despite all these attacks on our planet, the situation does not seem entirely hopeless. Indeed, the rhinoceros is not doing too badly. An article in the UK magazine *The Economist* even speaks of a 'rhinoceros revival'. Environmentalists will undoubtedly relate this good news to their tireless crusade. Their delight will be shared by many. However, another, unexpected – if not suspect – figure may well claim to have played a part in this encouraging revival: the financier. Such a claim begs an immediate question. On what grounds can a financier claim credit for involvement in an endeavour that seems so far remote from his daily concerns? On the grounds that, thanks to his creativity, seemingly diverging interests can be somehow realigned.

As a matter of fact, protecting nature is not an easy task. Developing countries often protest to environmentalists that they cannot give priority to the rhinoceros, or other equally endangered species and their natural habitat. Indeed, this may conflict with their daily efforts to combat poverty. Yet priorities of this kind are often imposed on poor countries, even when they seem contrary to the interests of their people or their economic well-being, at least in the short run. The vicious trade-off between the short-term struggle against poverty and the longer term fight for nature preservation seems unavoidable. This is precisely where modern international finance breaks in to circumvent the hitherto damaging trade-off. For instance, financiers have crafted an unusual financial product: the debt-for-nature swap. Most developing countries are highly indebted. They are scarcely solvent. Debt hangs over them like a sword of Damocles, discouraging even the most determined efforts to cope with their economic problems. As a result nature protection does not rank first on their agendas. The World Wide Fund For Nature (WWF) has launched an initiative designed to break this vicious circle. In 1989, it mandated NMB Bank to arrange an original transaction. As of 15 August 1989, the announcement of the transaction read as follows:

WWF World Wide Fund For Nature has completed a US$2,271,112.16 debt for nature conversion in the Republic of Zambia to finance, in cooperation with the Government of Zambia, the conservation and management of the Kafue Flats and Bangweulu Basin, the protection of Zambia's rhino and elephant populations, and to support conservation education activities and local conservation institutions in Zambia.

On another occasion, the WWF acquired a small part of Ecuador's external debt for a nominal value of US$9 million. It then agreed to waive repayment of this debt in exchange for a programme of rainforest protection. In other words, the WWF entered into a swap that exchanged debt for nature protection. Swaps are well-known instruments on international financial markets. They enable the exchange of currencies or interest rates. With the help of NMB Bank, the WWF has taken an innovative stance in using swaps to exchange a non-financial variable, namely nature, against a financial variable, namely debt. Of course, given the sheer size of the Third World debt, the amounts in question are still very modest. None the less, the principle is a compelling one. A financial instrument – a derivative, to use the jargon – is taken out of its normal arena, the financial markets, and utilised to help solve a problem which concerns us all.

This should inspire both U2 Irish rock singer Bono and Pope John Paul II in their Jubilee 2000 crusade[1] to obtain the straight cancellation of the Third World debt (Bono, 2000). The cause promoted by Jubilee 2000 is undoubtedly a noble one. It is predicated on the grounds that wealthy creditor nations should act generously and waive the debt burden of poor debtor nations. It may nevertheless entail some significant problems. Again, to use Bastiat's or Hazlitt's own words, the debt burden is what is seen. The unseen, however, may turn out to be even worse than the debt overhang problem. Indeed, a feel for generosity and compassion is at risk of triggering significant moral hazard issues. This is what Harvard University economist Robert Barro reminded Bono of in a *Business Week* article (Barro, 1999). A straight debt cancellation without any compensation may send mixed signals. For instance, indebted countries may

---

[1] A website is dedicated to this crusade: www.dette2000.org

argue that Jubilee 2000 applies also to them and decide to slow down economic and democratic reforms or even to default on their obligations. Debt relief would appear to come for free. In this respect the WWF has been more cautious in demanding nature protection compensation.

The rhinoceros, then, does not owe its survival solely to the vigilance of environmentalists. Financial markets have contributed also to its revival. Strangely enough, the Cornish or Breton fisherman seems to be in a more fragile position. One may even wonder whether the fisherman has actually become the victim of these same environmentalists, who criticise him for the mesh size of his nets and blame him for the over-exploitation of the seas and for the depletion of fish stocks. Richard Bronk, a City economist, notes that 'in Newfoundland some 35 000 fishermen have been put out of work by the collapse of the fishery in 1992' (Bronk, 1999). He attributes this fatal trend to over-fishing. Over this century, the world's fish catch may have increased an impressive twenty-fold. However, these mind-boggling statistics look like the tree hiding the forest. They do not shed any light on why our so-called modern societies end up blessing a weird bookkeeping that registers the rhinoceros on the credit side and the fisherman on the debit side. Environmentalists argue that the decline in the fishing industry is nothing to do with them. They accuse the free market ideology that, among other things, leads fishermen to catch fish at unsustainable levels. To paraphrase David E. Price, fishermen are at risk of simply becoming obsolete (Price, 1959). London School of Economics' John Gray claims that 'free markets have (also) weakened or destroyed (other) institutions on which social cohesion depends' (Gray, 1999). He goes as far as suggesting that the Utopia of the global free market may over time come to rival communism in the suffering that it inflicts! In a nutshell, global free markets, beefed up by international capital flows, are said to have become out of control, leaving countless casualties behind them.

Many people might find these arguments against the presumably wild world of free markets convincing, not least the fishermen themselves. The scenario is rather appealing. The crime is perfect and culprits will never be arrested. But, is this really a new story? To say the least, free markets have never had a good press. Their main agents, the financiers, have always been promised to hell. For instance, in medieval cathedral sculpture, the moneylender (the financier – or rather, the usurer – of the time) is represented as a criminal condemned to be pilloried. The usurer reaps a profit from something that does not belong to him. Indeed, interest profit is illegitimate because time belongs only to God (Le Goff, 1986). St Augustine denounced money lust as one of the three principal sins with power and sex lust. In the same vein, Charles Dickens' Scrooge does not help much in cleaning up the badly tarnished image of the financier (Dickens, 1843). The insatiable greed of free marketers is leveraged by the efficient machine of international finance, by the many modern Scrooges who can move quicksilver capital from one place to the other in a wink. Hence, the Cornish or Breton fisherman has become one of the hostages of this destructive scheme.

This interpretation of the paradox opening this first parable is too hasty by far. It establishes a division of responsibilities which, however attractive it may sound, distorts reality. Fishermen are victims, like the rhinoceros and many others, of the tyranny of the real economy, not the virtual economy[2] or international finance. They are caught up in what French sociologist Pierre Bourdieu (1994) calls 'a tragic mechanism', in which they may be doomed to permanent failure. All of them are 'in some way obliged to participate, in order to exist, in a game which demands of them immense effort and immense sacrifices'. This game is all the more daunting in that the fishermen have no control over the rules. They are caught more often than not in an infernal downward spiral: fish prices fall, their income declines, they become crippled by debt. They are going through the same kind of crisis as that affecting developing countries whose level of debt is giving so much concern to the banks in industrialised countries: low commodity prices, a fall in export revenue, the impossibility of keeping up with the relentless repayment schedule imposed by the creditor countries and major banks of the West. Thus the vicious circle of underdevelopment, inequality and poverty is formed and, as French economist Daniel Cohen (1994) has put it, 'poverty makes it impossible to invest in either people or machinery, thus perpetuating the original poverty'. This does not mean, however, that one should sink into pessimism. After all, who would have thought that the rhinoceros would one day underlie a financial derivative asset. The real economy is often hostile, but the virtual economy holds many promises.

A simple parable suffices to convey what is meant by the virtual economy. This parable is about the rhinoceros, the fisherman and the financier. It is an invitation to look more closely at how economic

---

[2] We use hereafter 'virtual economy' or 'virtual finance' as a convenient way to encompass capital markets and, more specifically, financial derivatives markets. Besides, this is usually the definition used by the detractors of capital markets.

factors affect our daily life. Fishermen tell us a painful economic story that everyone has to listen to. However, as we shall see, their story is revealing but not unique. Social security systems, pension schemes, labour markets, risk-sharing opportunities are other examples which deserve significant improvements. Whether deliberately or through negligence, we tend to condemn whole sections of our social and economic fabric to the scrap heap. For instance, Yale University economist Robert Shiller (1998) observes that 'the major economic risks that our society faces are dealt with individually: each person bears his or her own misfortunes'. He recognises that 'society does share some risks, such as risk of natural disaster, medical emergencies, or temporary unemployment'. However, it is fair to say that most of the risks threatening our standards of living are not shared. These standards of living are driven significantly by 'a game of chance', Shiller deplores. For instance, everything from the size of the corn crop to sales of soft drinks depends upon the prevailing weather conditions. Michael J. Mandel, economics editor of *Business Week* magazine, talks about 'the high-risk society' in which 'economic insecurity has become a fact of life for every worker and every business' (Mandel, 1996). Unfortunately, critics of the market economy and the financial markets ignore these obvious facts. They prefer to be prophets of doom and to complain about the law of the jungle of capitalism. They look at one side of the coin and overlook the other side. This is a rather strange attitude which is not conducive to any progress. It fails to ask the most relevant questions.

Indeed, why should one take for granted that fishermen or farmers have to be able to cope with volatile world prices, capricious weather as well as being skilled at their jobs? By trying to kill too many birds with one single stone, one ends up missing them all. The jack-of-all-trades becomes the master of none – to the detriment of society and the real economy as a whole. Unfortunately, these dysfunctions are frequent and costly. The hitherto proposed cures have been costly too. The usual course of action has been the introduction of large-scale programmes of subsidies and price guarantee. These turn out to be expensive measures which do not solve any of the real problems. Worse, they trigger the wrong responses, leading economic decision-makers on a downhill path. This is not to say that people facing difficulties should be refused help. Proper methods should first be designed, chief among them, new methods of risk-sharing. The primary objective should be to enable everyone to act according to his or her own capabilities, rather than suffering from the dire consequences of events over which he or she has no control. The challenge is to circumvent the tyranny of the real economy and its trail of risks by creating and deploying a whole range of instruments yielding better risk-sharing opportunities. In other words, more financial markets are needed!

The story of the Cornish or Breton fisherman is particularly instructive here. The recent troubles that have hit the fishing industry demonstrate clearly that subsidies are as efficient as a Sisyphean task. They do not provide any real solution to the basic problem and sooner or later they become unsustainable. Problems can hardly be resolved by 'spreading' them over collective shoulders. What then are Cornish or Breton fishermen struggling so passionately for? Their income; that is, a reasonable reward, a decent price, for the fish they catch. More to the point, they can no longer stand the current situation where highly volatile fish market prices jeopardise the future of their business. The fishermen have become victims whose fate is dictated by throws of the dice. Indeed, the fishermen are expected to run multiple risks every day, including risking their family incomes and their own lives. Is it fair to expect them to shoulder a burden of risks too heavy for them to bear? To borrow an analogy from the world of horse race betting: Cornish and Breton fishermen start the race with a severe handicap. They are aware of this. Indeed, they have organised for years some internal risk-sharing. They try to spread part of the risk burden among themselves by agreeing to index their respective earnings to the size of the catch. Hence, if the catch does not meet expectations, each fisherman accepts that he will take part of the hit. However, they are unable to share the other main risk, namely the price risk, with the rest of society: once the boat reaches the harbour and the fish is put up to auction, the price risk stays with the fishermen themselves. It is not shared with society. We enjoy tasting the fish on our plates, but choose to ignore the fate of the people who caught it. The intention is not to discard the fascination that was felt by French novelist Paul Morand (1937) when he wrote enthusiastically that 'risk is beautiful: there can be no great thoughts, no sublime actions without it, no independence, no liberalism'. He added that statistics, the efficient provision of collective security and the systematic mutualisation of risk gave rise to an Inca civilisation which had quite simply eliminated anxiety. Yet, it only took Pizarro and his conquistador adventurers, fleeing oppressive medieval Spain, to sweep away this tranquil centuries-old civilisation and take possession of its riches. Morand concludes that life is not worth living unless one is ready to roll the dice and accept their verdict, and then to bounce back more strongly. There is no question at all that Cornish or Breton fishermen, whether or not they have read Paul Morand, would fully agree with him. One does not become a fisherman by chance. It requires strong moral fibre and a great deal of effort and daring to 'harvest' the seas, venturing farther afield, whatever the weather. This risk is accepted knowingly because the fisherman has what it takes to cope with it. The sea is to be feared, but this is a freely chosen risk. Unfortunately, not all risks fall into this category and Paul Morand's perspective fails to take into account that not all risks are born equal in the eyes of an entrepreneur. Some of them cannot be monitored. Some others could be taken voluntarily but are not, or are no longer taken, because they carry with them unexpected hazards which may ruin the soundest business. The volatility of fish prices is without a doubt one such hazard.

Hence, the economy in which Cornish and Breton fishermen operate is truly tyrannical. It entails also pernicious effects: in the European Community, each fish price crisis is taken care of by throwing out a lifeline in the form of a programme of subsidies. Each programme is at best a tranquilliser until the next crisis. Yet, today, a whole panoply of instruments is available whose function is, for example, to allow the corporations to shield themselves against the gyrations of interest rates and exchange rates, the Kansas farmer to hedge the yo-yo movement of wheat prices and the rhinoceros to avoid extinction. So, how come the fisherman cannot hedge the volatility of fish prices over which he has no control? If fish prices fall the fisherman ends up in a bad fix. His income is deteriorating although he has still to reimburse the loans financing his boat and his business. To avoid such a double curse the appropriate answer is to engineer a financial instrument in the spirit of what has already been achieved for the benefit of the rhinoceros. The proper concept is indeed that of 'financial engineering'. Engineering is the implementation of mathematical and scientific knowledge to solve problems and to design useful and relevant products and services. For instance, civil engineers used their knowledge of materials and mechanics to build the bridge road connecting the Keys in Florida. According to Harvard Business School Professor of Finance, Peter Tufano (1996), 'the financial engineer's knowledge base is financial economics, or the application of economic principles to the dynamics of securities markets, especially for the purpose of structuring, pricing, and managing the risk of financial contracts'. Financial engineers incorporate the various objectives and constraints to produce the financial instrument with the appropriate cashflows. Such an engineering approach has been applied to the Third World debt to make this debt more compatible with the income fluctuations of commodity producing countries. By indexing the coupon and/or principal repayments to the price of commodities produced by Third World countries, financial engineers have designed an instrument whereby investors have agreed to carry part of the commodity price risk. Indeed, if, say, the price of cocoa dips, then the cocoa producing country reimburses less money to the investors. Hence, the pain of falling cocoa prices and export revenues is alleviated by the diminishing debt instalments. Following these examples, banks that grant loans to the fishing industry should think of indexing these loans to a suitable fish price index. When the index value rises, the interest rate charges rise at the same time. But this is precisely when the fisherman can best afford it. His income is rising. When the index value falls, so do the interest rate charges. Thus, the fisherman is freed from the vicious circle of fixed financial costs. Instead, his costs keep pace with the ups and downs of his income from fishing. Through this mechanism, the risk has been transferred from the fisherman to his bank. In the fifteenth century, the Medici family's bank was already operating a lending system along these lines. The French chronicler Philippe de Commynes held an investment account at the Lyon branch of the Medici bank (Braudel, 1979). The interest rate was indexed to the profits of the project in which his funds were invested. Eventually, Philippe de Commynes complained that the income he was receiving was too low: 'The said revenue is very meagre for me'. However, he knew the rules of the game. By giving up a fixed return on his investment, he had accepted a share of the risk in the hope of a higher future return.

But what can be done to ensure that the bank itself does not go bust when, say, fish prices fall? Some people, of course, will argue against this risk transfer precisely on the grounds that the bank would become highly vulnerable to the ups and downs in fish prices. However, in the current scenario, the harm has already been done. Indeed, how many fishermen do remain solvent when a crisis strikes? Banks, too, are victims – wittingly or not – of this volatility tyranny. All things considered, however, a loan indexation is preferable for the bank to the bankruptcy of its clients. Indeed, the bank is sensitive to fish prices even if its loans are not indexed. It is sensitive in a passive way: falling fish prices jeopardise the business of its clients, hence their ability to reimburse the loans. The bank would rather avoid cases where the fishermen default on their loans because of diving fish prices. A client alive is always better than a dead client!

What is needed though is a mechanism whereby the bank can also download its exposure to the gyrations of fish prices. This is precisely the role of futures and forward commodities markets (also called derivatives markets) where the prices of commodities are quoted daily for transactions that will take place three, six, nine or more months later. Just as the virtual economy is the natural extension of the real economy, a futures market is the logical development of a cash market. Instead of quoting a price for goods to be sold immediately, a futures or a forward market establishes prices for deferred sale. Thus, in parallel with a cash quotation for, say, tuna, a futures or a forward market would quote sale prices for tuna to be paid and delivered in three months, six months, nine months, and so on. In other words, operators have simultaneous access to a market where delivery and payment are immediate and to a market where delivery and payments are deferred to a pre-agreed known date in the future. This combination of cash and forward operations is not new. The famous French historian Fernand Braudel mentions the writings of a 'curious merchant', a Spanish Jew called Joseph de la Vega (1650–1692) who was astonished to learn that in Amsterdam 'herring was sold forward, before it was even caught, and cereals and other goods before they had begun to grow or been harvested' (de la Vega, 1688). The great commodity futures markets in America date from the nineteenth century. As far back as the seventeenth century, many transactions took place on forward markets in Amsterdam. The most famous example is the forward market in tulip bulbs. Farmers and flower growers had come to realise that, to cope with the uncertainties of the weather and the chance of natural disasters, it was better to be able to establish in advance a fixed price for their harvest. If a grain or a flower crop is not harvested yet, obviously it cannot be sold on the cash market: a real physical transaction is impossible. The only possibility is a virtual transaction; that is, sell today at a price (the forward price) and a date that are fixed in advance, a crop that has not yet been harvested. The delivery and the settlement will take place on the agreed date. In the course of so doing, farmers remove the price volatility from their income.

Since these first forward markets were introduced, they have been extended to numerous products: gold, silver, shares, currencies, interest rates, frozen prawns, sugar, cocoa, livestock, rice, soybeans, orange juice, potatoes, pork bellies, and so on. This long list shows that operators in a wide variety of sectors have understood the great advantages to be gained from the existence of a second marketplace for their products. Plenty has been written about the organisation of forward and futures markets. No matter what the product, the basic features of all these markets are identical. First of all, the transactions are either conducted on an over-the-counter basis (forward markets) or on official, organised markets (futures markets). In this last case it means that the transactions have to follow very strict rules which guarantee both that they are properly executed and that the operators are creditworthy. The contracts that are exchanged on futures markets are standardised in order to ensure the greatest possible market liquidity. The connection between a cash market and a futures market – between 'real' cash prices and 'virtual' forward prices – is checked and maintained continuously by financial operators called arbitrageurs. This is quite natural, after all: the same underlying product is involved, but with a double quotation, spot and forward. Obviously, these two quotations cannot drift apart and this is precisely the job of arbitrageurs to ensure that they do not.

The efforts that have gone into organising and standardising forward and futures markets are strong evidence of the interest of all the various parties concerned – producers, investors, manufacturers, speculators, public authorities – for efficient risk-transferring systems. Indeed, forward and futures markets are most useful to all the players, in that they perform two essential functions: the transfer of risks and the provision of information.

Forward and futures markets enable risk to be transferred. A bank granting a loan to a fisherman can afford to index the loan instalments to fish prices. This is so because the bank can sell its fish price exposure on the forward or futures fish market. Assume for the sake of simplicity that the loan is a one-year loan. If the fish price falls down at yearend, then the fisherman reimburses less and the bank is less profitable than expected. However, if the bank has sold a one-year forward contract on fish, its yearend position is much better. Indeed, at the end of the year, the bank will buy back its contract.[3] In this case, a profit will be registered: fish prices have dipped and the bank repurchases its fish contract at a lower price than the price at which it agreed initially to sell fish. Hence, its income loss is compensated by its gain on the forward market. The bank has provided the fisherman with a valuable function. It has removed the fish price risk from him. It can do so because the risk is then passed on to other players on the forward market. The risk does not disappear, however. It is still there in the economy but in another format. It has been cut into pieces bought and sold by numerous people. It is then less heavy to carry for each of them.

The banking transaction is not the only hedging scheme available to fishermen. Assume that a tuna fisherman is exposed to a drop in the

---

[3] The bank will not deliver fish! This is not its business. It will simply cancel its obligation by buying back the contract and paying or receiving the price difference, if any.

price of tuna. If the fall in price occurs between, say, the time when the fish is caught and when it is sold on the market, then the fisherman experiences a loss. If he is able to carry out a forward transaction, he can fix a price in advance which insures him against any untimely downturn in tuna prices. Therefore, he has transferred the risk. However, the global risk has not disappeared, but has simply been redistributed to the individual or institution most able to bear it. This could be a tuna fish canning factory whose risk position balances that of the fisherman. It could even be a professional speculator. For the canning factory, the fall in fish prices is good news: it means that business costs fall too. Any rise in fish prices is, on the contrary, bad news for the factory – especially if it is difficult to pass the increase through to the final customer. Through the futures or forward market, the fishermen can sell his fish to the factory on a forward basis. The factory becomes a forward buyer. If it happens that the price of tuna falls, then the fisherman loses the on-the-spot sale but recoups this loss on his forward transaction. His gain on the futures or forward market corresponds to the loss borne by the factory, which, however, has benefited from the lower prices on the cash market. Their respective incomes are levelled out and both are able to concentrate on their field of expertise without having to worry about chaotic prices. As an additional result, the forward market also makes it possible to reduce the burden of subsidies. Subsidies have perverse economic effects: they disturb the logic of prices, which then are less able to act as reliable signals, hence as incentives. In fact, subsidised prices encourage indolence. Subsidies are rarely good news and usually they have a strong political slant. Futures and forward markets, in contrast, are places where economic agents seize risk with both hands and invent effective methods of risk transfer.

The other valuable function of futures and forward markets is to deliver additional price information to the various decision-makers involved. Indeed, they make it possible to anticipate future prices of the commodities quoted on them over specific periods of time. For example, for a tuna canning factory, the simple fact of being able to observe not only what the price of tuna is today but also what it will be in three months is extremely valuable. It is a useful piece of information for planning purposes. The three-month forward price of tuna embodies information about what the cash price for tuna may be in three months. Indeed, the financial market is continually digesting all available information – supply, demand, weather and shipping forecasts, political background, environmental constraints and so on – and then releasing it in condensed form as the forecast price for tuna in, say, three or six months. The accuracy of this evaluation varies, of course, according to the quality of the information fed in by the market. One thing is clear though: through the futures and forward markets, economic agents can benefit from the time-series of prices that emerge from the aggregation of piecewise information that each of them gathers. This information-gathering task is also achieved thanks to the indispensable role of operators who are often disparaged in the press: the arbitrageurs who make sure that spot prices and forward prices stay in line, and the speculators. The speculators act as insurance companies. They agree to carry the risk of the counterparty wanting to offload it. Yet, they are accused of every kind of villainy. In his political economy course of 1895, Joseph Rambaud, a professor at the Law faculty of the Catholic University of Lyon, noted that 'the size of modern markets, the continual tendency towards a levelling-out between them, the ease of communications, all combine to rapidly correct any undue volatility in forward prices'. He added that 'it has been proposed that all forward markets be banned...', but 'that would be to go too far', he concluded, because forward markets 'are perfectly proper, and closely linked to real commercial deals, which they guarantee in such a way as to cancel out any excessive price differences'.

At this point, one basic question has to be asked: if the potential benefits of forward and futures markets are so obvious and the risk management concepts underlying them are fairly simple, why have they not already been put in place in the fishing sector? Doug Henwood, journalist at New York's radio station WBAI has strong views on this issue (Henwood, 1998). He argues that the social function of futures markets has a 'homey appeal', but that 'real life is different'. To support his claim, he quotes statistics and surveys showing that futures and forward markets 'are dominated by commercial interests' (which begs the question of why commercial interests would be harmful to society). A more serious argument is the one that he draws from the work of Cambridge University economist David Newberry (1989). According to Newberry, 'if prices are stabilized, but quantities remain unstable, incomes may be less stable than if prices were free to move in response to the quantity changes'. Hence, hedging would make society worse off than it would be if it remained unhedged. This is indeed an interesting observation which, however, brings water to the futures' mill. First, it is quite clear that any hedging strategy has to take into account the potential correlations between the various risks at hand, such as price and quantity. Secondly, Newberry's arguments give a strong rationale as to why markets for weather derivatives are blossoming. In a nutshell, the fisherman, the farmer, the travel agent can 'buy' the weather they want for their business. Too much rain may ruin a vineyard. To cope with this risk that translates into poor and low quality wine in small quantities, the wine producer now has the possibility of trading his rain exposure on the market. Hence, quantity risk related to weather conditions can also be shifted to the proper skillful hands.

Is it then a question of cultural resistance on the part of fishermen who are not keen to see the intrusion of market finance into their world? This explanation is not convincing at all. However paradoxical it may seem, the fisherman, too, is a man with wide market experience. A fish-market spot auction is the best example of a real, vibrant market, seething with action like the one described by French novelist Emile Zola in his wonderful book *L'Argent* (1911). No ingredient is missing: the auctioneer's skillful patter, the buzz of the bidding, the tense expressions, the tactics, the importance of timing, the need to act quickly and judiciously. The same intense market atmosphere is to be felt, for example, at the pig-breeders' market, or the cut-flower market. No, there is another explanation for this reluctance to embrace the virtual economy and its panoply of financial instruments. It is a more subtle one. According to Mancur Olson (1982) our democratic societies suffer from the growing proliferation of interest groups which hinder economic efficiency. In this respect, it is instructive to trace the route followed by the fish from the harbour to our plates. The large number of intermediaries along the way leads to a lack of transparency. The true price of the fish cannot be disentangled from the various tolls and commissions charged by this long chain of intermediaries. This chain is tyrannical because it introduces rigidities. Each link, instead of creating wealth, levies its own tithe along the way. In other words, each link in the chain is far from contributing real added value. The futures and forward markets are predicated on a rationale incompatible with this opaque and often parasitic system. They actually increase transparency. The operators on these markets, whoever they are, are obliged to 'place their cards on the table' and show clearly what their real contribution is. It is hardly surprising, then, that the interest groups concerned are in no great hurry to see a futures or a forward market spring up in their immediate environment! They even lobby against this.

It is the duty of society, nevertheless, to seize all opportunities offered by the virtual economy. The enemy is not virtual, but very much real. As Michael Mandel reminds us 'the preferred alternative is to offer everyone tools for managing uncertainty'. He adds that 'moving toward the financial market model, where people have choices about how much risk, and what kind of risks they want to take' is the right decision. Still, a lot of people are worried about the volume of transactions already going through the financial markets, especially the derivatives markets. Many commentators are sounding the alarm and expressing deep concerns when they see the volume of trading on futures markets overtake that on cash markets. In their view, the virtual economy is hypertrophied in comparison with the real economy and there is an ever greater risk that this bubble could burst at any moment. In his time, Joseph Rambaud noted, albeit without being worried, that 'as a result of speculative activities, it can happen, and in fact it does happen, that the transactions carried out relate to quantities of goods many times greater than are ultimately available for delivery'. These volumes traded on financial markets are a mere reflection of the tyranny exerted by the real economy. This is the other side of the coin. In fact, the large volume of trading on the virtual markets quite simply reflects the serious flaws of the real economy. Moreover, these volumes are small when properly measured against the risks that are still to be traded! It has never been easy to overthrow a tyrant. It takes a lot of effort. In a sense, financial markets are fomenting 'permanent coups d'état' whose purpose is to defeat the harmful consequences of economic risks.

An intelligent use of the virtual world can not only save the rhinoceros but also the fisherman and many other areas of economic society. One can 100% agree with Yale University economist, Robert Shiller (1998):

The sharing of economic risk is one of society's deepest concerns, and rightly so. Inequality of income and wealth is painful to see. Income and wealth determine who is served and who is servant, determine who may expect to live in comfort and health and who may not, determine who can pursue a fulfilling career or life plan or who cannot. To the extent that this inequality is created by pure luck, it is not only painful to see, but also a shame.

Rather than being one of the Four Horsemen of the Apocalypse, international finance and the virtual economy have the built-in ability to become a Guardian Angel.

THE PARABLE OF THE BLIND
PEARL-FISHER AND GERONIMO

In 1927, the famous journalist Albert Londres set sail for the 'Ebony Land'. He spent four months travelling all over French West Africa and French Equatorial Africa. In a scathing pamphlet (Londres, 1929), he remorselessly attacked the evils of white colonialism. As he said himself, the job of the journalist 'is not to please, nor to do harm, but to touch raw nerves'. A few years later, in 1931, he set off again, this time sailing down the Red Sea, visiting Jeddah, the Yemen, Dahlak and Djibouti, and Bahrain in the Gulf. An indefatigable observer (Londres, 1931), he criss-crossed the Red Sea aboard 'sambouks' in search of pearl-fishers. He was both fascinated and appalled at the painful itinerary, which began with the misery suffered by these men under the sea, and culminated in necklaces round the necks of beautiful women in the West. On the one hand, a richly adorned neck, on the other a poor devil attached to his rope, feverishly scraping the bottom of the sea. The dangers threatening Arab and Sudanese pearl-fishers were legion. Some were inescapable. Those who were particularly lucky could avoid others. There was no escape from perforated eardrums. Bronchitis was the common fate. Deafness and heart troubles were widespread. With luck, the pearl-fisher could hope to steer clear of the sawfish, the stingray, the electric ray and the shark. And on top of all this, there was still one final risk stalking the pearl-fisher: that of becoming blind. What hope was left for a fisherman who had gone blind? It is difficult imagine him groping along the seabed at a depth of 10 metres, searching for an oyster which he will never see again. Yet, what could he do, what else was he skilled at? The fatal blow had fallen on him. With the loss of his sight, his means of earning a living had disappeared forever.

However, this did not take into account the 'blind man's share'. At Dahlak, Londres discovered a really surprising custom. The pearl-fishers practised an unusual method of sharing out their harvest: one-third for the crew and themselves, one-third for the pearl dealers and one-third for the blind pearl-fishers. So, a proportion of the pearls went to compensate those who had lost their sight in the quest for them. And this proportion was immutable. 'The blind men did not have lawyers, their share was never in danger', Londres noted. No one would have dreamt of cheating the blind, of profiting by their infir-mity. Every pearl-fisher had total confidence in this insurance, which one day might come to his aid too. Every blind man had total con-fidence in those who were entrusted with the task of calculating his compensation in pearls and ensuring that it was paid to him. Londres noted ironically, 'Our own pension schemes were introduced long after the blind pearl-fishers' one-third share.'

Today, for many people, irony has understandably given way to unease. How is it that institutions as prestigious as Lloyd's of London and Barings Bank in the United Kingdom, as well as the savings and loans banks, Executive Life, Orange County in the United States, Herstatt Bank, Metallgesellschaft in Germany, Crédit Lyonnais, GAN in France, and Yamaichi in Japan appear to be less reliable than an informal collection of Greek, Arab or Sudanese pearl-fishers scraping the bottom of the Red Sea in the hope of finding pearls? As one

French politician once quipped, promises seem to bind only those to whom they are given. Yet, Julian Barnes (1995) notes that the British used to claim proudly that Lloyd's of London was 'as safe as the Bank of England'. Together with Rolls Royce and Saville Row, Lloyd's kept the British flag flying high. Today, the flag is at half-mast and the Lutine Bell is tolling not just for lost ships but also for the august institution in whose underwriting room it has hung since 1857. To witness such important symbols losing their reputation is bound to create a sense of anxiety. Some regard it as the price that has to be paid for the omnipresence of financial markets, for the relentless pursuit of profit. The appetite for fast money, they say, leads to the worst kind of blunders. According to French philosopher Jean Chesneaux (1996), the economy is now set in 'a time frame that has become blurred, equivocal, virtual'. Chesneaux notes, with some apprehension, that 'the markets gamble on the future price of shares, the exchange rate of currencies, interest rates' and that 'they want to buy future goods on credit, by trading in virtual loans which do not exist and never will exist'. UK economist Susan Strange echoes the same concerns in her book entitled *Casino Capitalism* (1997). It seems, if we are to believe Chesneaux and Strange, that the solid promises made by the Red Sea pearl-fishers have been replaced by a never-ending flow of virtual promises that risk turning the world into 'Planet Las Vegas'.

It is true that the current structure of financial intermediation can lead managers of banks, savings institutions and insurance companies to take considerable risks. The temptation of the casino is unfortunately there, and, paradoxically, prudential banking and insurance regulations often lend force to it.

There is a neat term for this temptation, which has led to the downfall of numerous financial institutions: 'to gamble for resurrection'. This expression has been coined in the United States to describe the demise of savings and loans associations. Resurrection, however, has turned into a real disaster, a descent into hell, a welter of costly failed promises. The commotion caused by these collapses, although painful, should not, however, lead to a superficial analysis of the facts. The detour around by the Red Sea and the pearl-fishers is highly instructive in this respect. With this in mind, let us return to Dahlak and add some new chapters to Albert Londres's report.

Let us assume that the pearl sharing has just been taking place. The blind pearl-fishers have just received the one-third of the catch of pearls that is their due. They could sell them directly and thus cash in some ready money. They could also decide to save them and to deposit all or part of these precious pearls with a financial institution. In fact, a banker puts a proposition to them, saying that he can make a profit on their pearl assets, which he values at £9000. In exchange for the pearls, this banker promises to return their precious capital one month later plus interest. To convince the pearl-fishers of the attractiveness of his proposal, the banker 'guarantees' them an interest rate slightly higher than otherwise available. The blind pearl-fishers, enthusiastic about the proposal, entrust their pearls to the banker without hesitation. It turns out that the banker has personal capital of £2000. Keen to diversify his own assets, he decides to assign half of his fortune, £1000, to the bank which he has just created for collecting and managing pearl deposits. Thus, the bank starts off with £10 000 available for investment. The banker must decide on an investment strategy. The one he opts for is the following. He goes to Monte Carlo and gambles all the resources at his disposal, his own and those of the bank, at the casino. Being an astute gambler, he stakes his personal funds, £1000, on the red and the bank's £10 000 on the black. He is perfectly aware of the possible outcomes of such a ploy. If the colour on which a gambler has placed his money 'comes up', he pockets twice his initial stake. For the pearl-fishers, this investment strategy is extremely risky. From the point of view of the banker – who is also the shareholder of the bank – it is much less so. In fact, if the red comes up, the bank's position is extremely simple: the whole of the managed fund is lost, and bankruptcy is declared. The pearl-fishers would have been better advised to hang on to their assets. The banker's promise will obviously not be kept. By contrast, the banker acting in a personal capacity doubles his stake, £2000, namely his initial stake grossed up by his gain. For him, the outcome of this investment strategy is neutral. He gains nothing, but loses nothing. He is back to square one. He can therefore play again, after gathering together new funds. If black is the winning colour, the banker loses the £1000 that he owned personally. His financial institution, how-ever, wins the jackpot, collecting £20 000. He returns the promised sum, principal plus interest to the blind pearl-fishers. He then gains the reputation of a shrewd banker. Indeed, the banker is rewarded twice for his risky strategy. By putting his institution, and therefore the pearl-fishers, at a considerable risk, he has managed to make himself much richer and to deliver the promised amount of money to his clients.

This 'Monte Carlo' temptation is a simple but fair description of the course taken by many financial institutions towards ever more risky investments. It has been the cause of many well-publicised troubles. One objection may be raised against the Monte Carlo strategy, though. If the bank goes bust, it will no longer be able to attract new pearl-fishers, that is, new clients. The pearl-fishers would not let themselves be duped a second time. As a matter of fact, they might. All that would be needed is a deposit guarantee provided, say, by a dedicated insurance fund or by the State itself. Thus, if red wins, the bank cannot honour its commitments. In that case, the guarantor intervenes and indemnifies the blind pearl-fishers. Prudence is thus removed. The pearl-fishers can be metaphorically as well as actually blind. They have no reason either to worry or to monitor the banker's business methods. Whatever happens, their deposits are safe. They are guaranteed by the State.

But what has the banker really done? Is he simply a scoundrel motivated by fraudulent intentions? Or is his behaviour perfectly rational, given the environment in which he operates? The banker has invested £1000 as shareholder. In other words, he owns slices of ownership in the bank. But, this ownership is characterised by a specific provision, namely limited liability. If the bank collapses, he is not obliged to make up for the deficit. At worst, he loses his own initial stake. In other words, his personal wealth outside the bank is ring-fenced and cannot be used to compensate deposit-holders; the pearl-fishers have granted him the possibility of defaulting on his obligations. Hence, limited liability is nothing but an option to default. The UK magazine *The Economist* describes limited liability as 'the key to industrial capitalism' (*The Economist*, 1999). Limited liability laws were promulgated in America in 1811 and in the UK in 1854. The main idea was to encourage shareholders to put their money at risk while protecting their private property. The limited liability provision implies that shares can be viewed as a call option on the assets of the corporation issuing the shares. If the assets are valuable enough to repay the claim-holders, shareholders do so and pocket the difference as a reward for their investment. If things go wrong and shareholders are unable to repay the claim-holders, they are allowed to walk away. The creditors seize the assets. Hence, the repayment due to the claim-holders acts as a threshold which assets must reach if bankruptcy is to be avoided. In the financial jargon, such a threshold is called an exercise price. It is then easy to understand why the Red Sea banker decided to go for highly volatile 'Monte Carlo' strategies. If black wins, everything is fine. If red wins, the bank goes bankrupt and the banker can walk away under the protection of the limited liability provision.

The pearl-fishers are betrayed. The word of the Red Sea banker is not his bond. Their respective incentives are not perfectly aligned, especially if the pearl deposits are not guaranteed. To use the finance jargon, the banker is 'long' a limited liability option to walk away (whose underlying assets are the assets in which he has invested the pearls) while the pearl-fishers are 'short' the same option. The key insight here is that the one who owns the option may be incited to increase the volatility, the risk of the assets underlying this option. Hence, the one who is short the option is at risk and should find ways of monitoring the behaviour of his counterparty. Similar stories are not rare. They can be found in rather unexpected places.

This is indeed a lesson that the legendary Apache chief Geronimo has learnt to his detriment (Geronimo, 1970). During the nineteenth century, he and his companions fought the US Cavalry rather successfully. Sometimes, they agreed to sign peace treaties. Geronimo's word was his bond and he trusted, in particular, US Cavalry General Crook. However, some other fellows were not as trustworthy and had a strong incentive not to have peace too soon. A smuggler, going by the name of Tribolet, and his so-called 'Tucson clique' were making a living out of the presence of the US Cavalry in Arizona. The more soldiers, the better for them. The more troubles, the stronger their activity. Their business consisted of selling, often illegally, cattle, horses, spirits, ammunition, and so on. In 1881, after having done battle with the Yankee and the Mexican armies, Geronimo, his fellow chiefs Juh and Nachez and their people agreed to live on the reserve of San Carlos. Tribolet and his men were selling them a lot of whisky. One day in September 1881, the Apaches had drunk more than usual. Taking advantage of their trance, Tribolet convinced them that Geronimo and the other chiefs would soon be jailed and executed. Geronimo, Juh, Nachez and 74 warriors decided to leave the reserve and to resume the war against the palefaces. The US Cavalry response was immediate as expected by Tribolet. More troops were sent and General Wilcox was ordered to chase and arrest Geronimo. This was extremely good news for Tribolet and his clique. More money was to be expected. To use the financial jargon, they had increased the value of their option on future business by creating additional turmoil. Besides, the evidence provided by University of Oklahoma historian, Dan L. Thrapp (1964), supports this interpretation. Geronimo was convinced that Tribolet had told him the truth. He was sure that soldiers were chasing him to hang him.

Geronimo and the Red Sea pearl-fishers are companions in misfortune. Although their word is their bond, they are betrayed by forces that seem stronger than they are. As a matter of fact, their respective situations are quite similar. They trust a counterparty whose incentive is to create volatility; whose best policy is to implement a 'Monte Carlo' strategy. More risk, more noise means potentially higher profits for this counterparty. Following this strategy, the Red Sea banker ends up better off; the Tucson clique ends up doing more business.

Nevertheless, to protect deposit-holders, like the pearl-fishers, against such misbehaviours, regulatory authorities have introduced some safeguarding mechanisms in the form of guarantees. Unfortunately, the results can be disastrous, as already mentioned. Indeed, if a third party, say, the State, guarantees pearl deposits, then the dire consequences of the highly volatile strategies are not even borne by the pearl-fishers. The guarantor institution, whether it is a special fund or the State itself, acts as a safety valve. The danger of this is obvious: pearl-fishers have no incentives either to behave prudently or to monitor the banker's strategies. The banker has the proper set of incentives to maximise the volatility of the bank's investments. In the course of doing so, he magnifies the value of his limited liability option to the potential detriment of the deposit-holders.

This system is perverse and pernicious. It means that pearls and, more generally, deposits are naturally attracted to the most risky and most precarious institutions, which are the ones offering the most appealing returns on investment. For the depositor, the risk is nil since the deposited funds are guaranteed. In a sense, they have nothing to lose and may expect above-market returns. So why worry? Depositors would certainly be more vigilant if their deposits were not insured in this way. In some cases, deposits may even be protected by a 'costless' guarantee. The French banking system – and this will probably also apply to the insurance system in the near future – exemplifies this. If one bank defaults on its obligations, then the others are called on to fill the gap. In situations where the State, directly or indirectly, acts as guarantor, it plays very much the role of the Good Samaritan. In the recent past, the French 'horror' stories of Crédit Lyonnais (sometimes nicknamed Débit or Crazy Lyonnais), GAN and other state-owned firms were a perfect illustration of 'go for broke' strategies. Since the State has deep pockets, there is no reason not to implement 'Monte Carlo' strategies. If these strategies are successful, they will be hailed as a stroke of genius. If, however, they yield heavy losses, the State will simply be asked to do its duty and divide the funds among citizens.

Unfortunately, the supervisory authorities and the government very often encourage this reckless course of action themselves. Indeed, economic history is punctuated with financial casualties where the State has more than its share of responsibility. For instance, the story of the US savings and loan institutions (hereafter S&Ls) was so appalling that the American economist Lawrence White (1991) has referred to it as a debacle. Doug Henwood, journalist at New York's radio station WBAI, goes as far as writing that 'no book on modern finance would be complete without a look at one of the greatest monetary disasters of all time, the savings and loans debacle of the 1980s' (Henwood, 1998). Estimates of the cost of rescuing the US S&Ls were repeatedly revised upwards. The total rose from US$50 billion when the Bush administration intervened to about US$500 billion. These figures are staggering, especially for the American tax-payer who must be flabbergasted to discover that the savings and loans problem dated back almost 20 years. Back in 1981 most of the savings banks should have been closed down on the basis of their true market value. Had the boil been lanced in 1984, the collapse would have cost only US$20–US$40 billion, according to some experts: a paltry amount compared with the colossal total it then reached.

S&Ls started in the nineteenth century as mutual savings banks that pooled peoples' savings to finance home mortgage loans. The roots of their debacle are to be found in the dual layer of protection which allowed these institutions to prosper from the early 1930s until the mid-1970s; namely, the ceiling on the interest rate paid on saving and time deposits, known as Regulation Q, and the guarantee of these deposits. Regulation Q was originally designed to prevent banks from competing with one another by paying higher interest to deposit-holders. The objective was to ban banks like the 'Red Sea bank'. It enabled S&Ls to collect cheap short-term savings and to grant fixed-rate long-term mortgage loans. They enjoyed fat margins that were quite stable because they were insulated from competition. During this period, running a savings and loans institution was considered an easy task. It boiled down to following the '3–6–3 rule': borrow at 3%, lend at 6% and start playing golf at 3 o'clock! On top of Regulation Q, deposits were (and still are) guaranteed in return for an insurance premium paid to the Federal Savings and Loans Insurance Corporation. The aim was to protect and reassure depositors. The guarantee was introduced to avoid outbreaks of panic, bank runs and the danger of a local bank's collapse rocking the whole financial system.

Unfortunately, these regulatory measures turned out to be very weak and artificial safeguards against the considerable interest rate risk exposure that arose from the savings banks' activities as lenders and borrowers. As long as interest rates remained relatively stable, the financial health of the savings and loans banks was assured. The imbalance between their assets (long-term residential mortgages) and their resources worked in their favour. However, the rise in interest rates following the first oil price shock of 1973 and the change in the Federal Reserve Board's monetary policy altered the financial landscape drastically. The interest rate hikes provoked massive cash outflows which the S&Ls had no means of resisting. Indeed, they were not allowed to deliver better deposit rates because of Regulation Q. Hence, depositors were attracted by investments offering far better returns. In order to withstand the competition represented by these investment opportunities, the banks and the S&Ls managed in 1979 to persuade the monetary authorities and the Congress to phase out Regulation Q. The consequence was disastrous. The S&Ls had operated year after year in a protected environment. They were unable to withstand the surging wave of interest rate risk that now threatened to overwhelm them. Their main assets – mortgages granted at low interest rates – were tied up for a very long term, 30 years on average. Therefore, the return on these assets could not keep pace with the increase in their cost of funding. Moreover, the management of these banks made things worse through incompetence, although it must also be recognised that it was difficult for them to be at the cutting edge of investment strategy given the numbing effect of regulations that provided no encouragement whatsoever in this direction. The S&Ls saw their profits decline rapidly and eventually they went into the red. As a result, the market value of their net worth melted like snow under the sun.

The damage caused by the interest rate gyrations was particularly severe in the case of the S&Ls which, unlike the commercial banks, were initially not authorised to offer mortgages at variable interest rates. By the time they were permitted to do so, in the early 1980s, interest rates had soared to record peaks. This chaotic course of events is a rather tragic illustration of regulatory laxity. Worse, the S&Ls were neither encouraged nor authorised to use new financial instruments, derivatives markets, as risk management tools.

Confronted with this financial mess, the authorities encouraged the S&Ls to 'gamble for resurrection'. Columbia University Professor of Finance, Franklin R. Edwards, recognises that 'banks have had an incentive to take excessive risks because of federal deposit insurance and de facto "too-big-to-fail" policies, which eliminate incentives for depositors to monitor banks and to penalise them for taking excessive risks' (Edwards, 1996). The pearl-fisher syndrome is indeed at work but on a massive scale. Concurrently with the deregulation of interest rates, the savings and loans banks' sphere of activity was extended beyond that of residential mortgage providers. Thanks to the Garn–St Germain Act of 1983 they were authorised to invest in more lucrative assets. However, mere financial logic indicates that this increase in profitability can be obtained only at the price of higher risks. S&Ls started selling commercial mortgages and investing in 'junk bonds'. These notorious bonds are characterised by a significant default risk. Indeed, firms that are trying to turn around their business or new firms whose business does not yet have much visibility usually issue them. In exchange, they yield a high coupon. As a matter of fact, the high coupon is the fair compensation for granting the share-holders of the issuing firms the option to walk away. Back to Dahlak again. Like the pearl-fishers, the S&Ls went short limited liability options. Everyone at the time was betting on spectacular profits that they hoped would enable the S&Ls to get out of the red. Thus, as insult is sometimes added to injury, default risk was now added to the interest rate risk. Unfortunately, red came out. With the plummeting oil prices in 1986 default risk materialised. It dragged down commercial real estate prices in the southern states of the United States. Many commercial mortgages had been extended to small oil companies, which had also been diversifying into commercial property. Because of the fall in their oil revenues, they were unable to meet their financial commitments. Then, the recession and the fall in property prices in the northeast of the United States triggered new savings and loans casualties. Moreover, with the American recession at the end of the 1980s, many firms that had issued junk bonds earlier ended up defaulting on them.

The authorities were strongly at fault in this reckless financial mismanagement. They allowed the 'Monte Carlo' process to continue. Worse, from 1981 onwards, the rate of failures began to accelerate. The guarantee fund itself ran into severe difficulties. It had too much to repay. The Federal Deposit Insurance Corporation (FDIC) then decided simply to mask the S&Ls' financial nightmare. It used cosmetics: it changed the accounting rules by switching from the standard Generally Admitted Accounting Principles (which are far from perfect) to Regulatory Accounting Principles. Many institutions that ought to have been declared bankrupt, had they gone through a fair audit of their net worth, were declared solvent by some kind of accounting magic. This miraculous return to financial health was unfortunately only skin-deep.

Some observers have attributed the S&L debacle, or at least its worsening, to the greed and gluttony of Wall Street in the 1980s. *Liar's Poker*, the best-selling book written by ex-Salomon Brothers bond trader Michael Lewis, is full of anecdotes where traders are playing games to the detriment of S&Ls (Lewis, 1989). These stories are also echoed in Doug Henwood's book *Wall Street*. This is rather unfair and, to say the least, an unwarranted generalisation. Stories about greedy golden boys sell well and they may even contain some elements of truth. They are, however, far from giving the full landscape. This would be too easy, too convenient. As shown by thrift expert Robert Litan, the S&L debacle was the result of a rather explosive cocktail combining interest rate risk, inflation, moral hazard, 'Monte Carlo' strategies and political cowardice and regulatory mess. Unfortunately, by acting the 'Monte Carlo' way politicians were convinced that they were buying time and that time would erase the previous mistakes.

Another solution was never explored at the time. It would have been a viable compromise even if it would not have solved everything. The main problem for the savings and loans banks was that of matching their variable-rate, mostly short-term, deposits with their fixed-rate, generally long-term, mortgage loans. Indeed, to keep things simple, it may be difficult to commit to pay variable coupons when fixed coupons are received on mortgage loans. Financial engineers have designed interest rate swaps to cope with this kind of risk management issue. These instruments make it possible to alter the 'financial identity' of financial assets. Through such swaps, a fixed-rate loan can be transformed into a variable-rate loan and vice-versa. Hence, even though market or regulatory conditions were imposing some tough business constraints on S&Ls, they could have defeated them by using proper financial derivatives such as swaps. In the course of doing so, they would have alleviated the pains inflicted by risks and regulation on their balance sheets and cash flows. Unfortunately, at the time, 'virtual' instruments were not in such widespread use as they are today. And, even if they had been actively traded, the odds that regulators would have penalised or banished their use by S&Ls would have been fairly high.

In a humorous short pamphlet, Jacques-Gilbert Ymbert (1825), a high-ranking French official in the first half of the nineteenth century, praised 'the dreadful, execrable art of running into debts, and the still more execrable art of never repaying them'. His tongue-in-cheek proposition was that incurring debts and never repaying them was the very foundation of social order. His work was addressed to 'respectable gentlemen'. It is to be feared that many of the managers of our financial institutions have been tempted by the status of 'respectable gentlemen'. The martyrdom of the American S&Ls is, in this context, almost a caricature. That of the insurance companies, perhaps even more so.

In fact, the story of the insurance companies has been so turbulent that some journalists have actually asked a rather paradoxical question: 'Should one take the risk of insuring oneself?' That was the surprising headline that appeared in an issue of the weekly business magazine *La Vie Française* in 1976. Some 20 years later, the same question is still topical. The number of insurance companies across the world that have defaulted on their obligations has grown significantly. At the beginning of the 1980s the first worrying signs began to appear in the

United States. Competition between financial institutions grew fiercer. It also changed register. Like their S&L colleagues the American insurance companies were directly affected by these upheavals, as were their policyholders. As a result, insurance companies had to offer flexible contracts, which made it easier to attract clients' savings. The insurance companies included appealing provisions in their policies: guaranteed rates of return, surrender options, policy loan options, and so on. The result was disastrous: 19 US companies failed in 1987, 40 in 1989 and 58 the following year.

Although the US insurance market is very fragmented, it would be wrong to think that these bankruptcies hit only the smaller life insurance companies. Large companies, such as Mutual Benefit Life and First Capital, also succumbed. Major companies were obliged to file for Chapter 11. Once again, promises were not kept. The blind pearl-fisher's share was hit hard. But here again, one should not jump to hasty conclusions. Looking for a 'convenient' scapegoat is just as pointless as it was in the case of the S&Ls. The root of these problems runs very deep and, at the risk of disappointing the financial markets' disparagers, cannot be attributed to the erring ways of an unbridled financially dominated economy.

In fact, for the past 50 years, American life insurance companies have had to operate in a climate of intense competition. In particular, they have been faced with the emergence of pension funds that have grabbed part of their market share. The reason for the insurance companies' loss of market share is to be found in their balance sheets. Every premium received from a client is invested in financial assets, whose cash flows are intended to honour the commitments made to the policyholder. The supervisory authorities, as a general rule, are very strict about the composition of the companies' investment portfolios. Until 1951, American life insurance companies were not authorised to hold equities. This restrictive regulation was then gradually relaxed. By contrast, the pension funds never had any restrictions on their equity investments. Taking advantage of a very favourable equity market during the 1950s and 1960s, the pension funds invested in them on a massive scale and were able to post very attractive returns. The life insurance companies were compelled to hold portfolios with a much more traditional structure, essentially consisting of investments in bonds and real estate. As a result, the performance of the pension funds surpassed that of the equities.

The economic climate in the late 1970s did not help the already tight situation in which the life insurance companies found themselves. Interest rates rose sharply, inflation soared. Policyholders were no longer confident that the return on their life insurance savings would be as high as they had expected. They wanted to benefit from the higher interest rates, and were looking for more profitable products. The life insurance companies' sales staffs wasted no time in getting the message across to their top management. The life insurers introduced new ranges of products in order to make policies more flexible and more responsive to changes in interest rates. All these new products had two features in common: a guaranteed return and a bonus pegged to the performance of the asset portfolio of the insurance company. The policyholder was therefore guaranteed to receive a minimum return and to benefit from the growth in the financial markets.

Faced with relentless competition from other insurance companies and from other financial intermediaries, the life insurers also played the card of maximum flexibility. They introduced numerous new clauses in their policies: along with guaranteed minimum returns, they offered the possibility of early redemption at any time (surrender options), of borrowing against policies at a fixed rate of interest (policy loan options), of extending the maturity of the policy, etc. These provisions were, of course, very attractive to clients. However, they also turned into looming problems that jeopardised the companies' balance sheets. This was particularly true of the guaranteed return and the surrender option. On the one hand, if interest rates were to drop, the company would end up unable to match the guaranteed return. If, on the other hand, interest rates went up, policyholders might be tempted to exercise their surrender option and invest their savings in higher yielding opportunities. The insurance company would have to face a massive cash outflow at a time when the value of its assets had fallen in response to the higher interest rates. This last risk is not just a theoretical one: the US insurance company Executive Life had to cope with a tidal wave of surrenders totalling US$3 billion over a period of less than six months. At the time, its portfolio was melting like snow under the sun.

Another example of flexibility was the inclusion of a clause giving policyholders the option to borrow from their insurer, using the capital of their policy as collateral. For the insurer, this could turn out to be very dangerous if the borrowing rate was fixed for the whole duration of the policy. Following an interest rate rise, policyholders are naturally tempted to exercise their right to borrow: they can borrow at a low rate and invest their borrowed money at markedly better rates elsewhere. For instance, the size of policy loans (as a percentage of assets) doubled between 1965 and 1981.

The quest for market share also meant seeking financial investments capable of performing better than those of one's competitors. In order to make their policies attractive, the life insurance companies started their quest for yield. However, financial theory and plain good sense warn that there is a price to be paid for such returns. The return that an investor receives depends on the risk taken. Generally speaking, the riskier the investment, the higher its expected return. For example, over a long period, an equity investment on the stock exchange will yield more than an investment on the bond or money market. But equity is a riskier investment than bonds. Moreover, should the company fail, the absolute priority rule stipulates that shareholders are repaid once all the other claim-holders have been reimbursed.

To enhance the policyholders' return, insurance companies invested in commercial mortgages and junk bonds. Until the end of the 1980s, these proved to be very lucrative investments with very few defaults. Dazzled by this potential, some life insurance companies invested up to 60% of their assets in these high-risk investments.

The years 1988 and 1989 marked a turning point. The global recession made life much more difficult and there was a growing number of bankruptcies in the property sector, while the junk bond market reached its lowest level at the end of 1990. In a time span of 15 months, the simultaneous fall in these two markets cost the American life insurance companies a staggering US$100 billion.

The turbulence in the markets was accompanied by massive media coverage. For many commentators, it symbolised the end of the 'golden eighties' and their villains like the film *Wall Street*'s Gordon Gekko. In April 1990, after the demise of the leading underwriter of junk bonds, Drexel Burnham, the inventor of these bonds, Michael Milken, pleaded guilty in court. The losses incurred by the life insurance companies on their investments in junk bonds came under scrutiny. This obsession with junk bonds is slightly surprising, given that the fall in this market was only one-third the size of that in the US real estate market. Indeed, it seems to be generally agreed now that the total cost of the American property crisis can be evaluated at US$3500 billion. By way of comparison, the October 1987 equity market crash on Wall Street washed out 'only' US$500 billion. However, equities and junk bonds are obviously more flashy and newsworthy than real estate regardless of the bigger losses incurred – the bursting of a so-called finance bubble (where financial derivatives were hardly involved) made much sexier headlines.

The misfortunes of the American life insurance companies are not a new phenomenon created as a result of the reckless virtual economy. In fact, during the depression of the 1930s, insurers has already faced the impact of heavy capital losses on asset values, early surrenders and policy loans. Their reaction at the time is of great interest. Forty life insurance companies (of the 300 in operation at the time) went bankrupt following the crash of 1929. In 1931 and 1932, one million policyholders hit by the recession used their surrender or policy loan options (for economic reasons rather than to obtain better terms). Faced with an increased inability to meet their obligations, leading insurers decided, in February 1933, to hold a meeting in

New York. Also attending this meeting, which was held in conditions of absolute secrecy, were representatives from the supervisory authorities, the insurance commissioners of 19 States. During this meeting, two radical measures were adopted. First, the insurers managed to convince the commissioners of the need to declare legal suspension of payments from March to September 1933, as had been done for the banks. The main difference lay in the length of the standstill agreement: while the American government suspended banking payments for one week, insurers were given a six-month breathing space. Secondly, the value of many securities held in asset portfolios had dropped to such an extent that many life insurers were forced to file for bankruptcy. The insurers' solution was to window-dress their balance sheets by changing the accounting rules. As a result, assets were no longer booked at market value (too low at the time) but rather at acquisition value (i.e. much higher). Accounting creativity was employed to hide the latent losses, a device that was again used during the S&L crisis. Some things do not seem to change! The rise and fall of Executive Life in the 1980s attests it.

Back in the 1980s, Executive Life was a symbol of both the glory and the decline of this sector; or, as Jacques-Gilbert Ymbert would say, of the art of making promises and not keeping them. In April 1991, the supervisory authorities of the State of California seized the company. To date, this is the biggest ever case of bankruptcy of a US insurance company. However, this outcome took a lot of people by surprise. Between 1974 and 1988, Executive Life enjoyed extra-ordinary growth, thanks to the stamina of its president, Fred Carr. He succeeded in lifting the company to the 15th place, in terms of the standard measure of assets under management, from a lousy 355th place in 1974. In 1988 the business magazine *Fortune* ranked it third in terms of profitability. When the supervisory authorities seized the company, they discovered that 65% of its assets were invested in junk bonds. In fact, it had one of the largest junk bond portfolios in the United States. The high return earned by this portfolio allowed Executive Life to conduct an aggressive market share conquest. This 'Monte Carlo' strategy took the company over the precipice, and meanwhile, thousands of 'blind pearl-fishers' had been seduced. In January 1990 alone, its stock fell by 65.4%. The collapse of Executive Life was closely linked to the debacle in the junk bond market. However, as we have already seen, in addition to the plummeting value of its assets, the company had to cope with a massive and fast wave of policy surrenders in the order of US$3 billion, a phenomenon fuelled by the intense media coverage. Again, the wrong colour came up and the players went broke.

The story of Executive Life is a little like that of the frog who wanted to be as big as an ox. In this fable, the ancient Greek writer of tales Aesop (1906) berates a frog for being so foolish.

As a huge over-grown Oxe was grazing in a Meadow, an old envious Frog that stood gaping at him hard by, call'd out to her little ones, to take Notice of the Bulk of that monstrous Beast; and see, says she, if I don't make myself now the bigger of the two. So she strain'd once, and twice, and went still swelling on and on, till in the conclusion she forc'd herself, and burst.

The tyranny of size does not affect only Aesop's frog. Many company executives succumb to the relentless pursuit of turnover, to the ceaseless capture of market share. This tyranny is underpinned, moreover, by the very foolish conviction that a large company cannot be left bankrupt. 'Too big to fail' is the term often used. It is in fact the same line of argument that applies to the convulsions that shook the prestigious Lloyd's of London. English novelist Julian Barnes gives an amusing description of the hot discussions between Lloyd's and the 'Names' (Barnes, 1995)[1]

Lloyd's: 'Here is your bill.'

Names: 'Can't pay, won't pay.'

Lloyd's: 'You are legally bound to pay, under contract, so pay up.'

Names: 'We accuse you of negligence in the management of our business.'

Lloyd's: 'Pay now, accuse later.'

Names: 'No, we are accusing now and will pay later, and only if the judgment is in your favour.'

Lloyd's: 'If you don't pay up now, the market might collapse.'

Names: 'That's not our problem.'

Lloyd's: 'If we collapse, policyholders will have to be paid first, and there will be nothing left for you; the only way for you to come off well is to make sure Lloyd's continues to exist. So pay up.'

Names: 'No chance.'

Lloyd's: 'You're bluffing.'

Names: 'No, it's you who are bluffing.'

Size is not the right concept to be given priority to. Expertise and talent are the right ones. Having the right expertise does not mean

---

[1] The Names are individuals who gamble their personal wealth in exchange for collecting Lloyd's insurance premiums. In the case of very big claims, the Names are called on to make good any deficit with their own money; their responsibility is therefore unlimited.

and will never mean having to be as big as an ox. By selling highly flexible policies, the American life insurers accepted, voluntarily or involuntarily, new risks that they were not used to. They sold options (to surrender, to borrow, etc.) to their clients. Such a strategy is not wrong in itself. The error lies in the fact that the insurers, blinded by the pursuit of size, did not take the time to manage the policyholders' options properly. Worse still, they exacerbated the situation by investing in assets that were incompatible with the risk management of these options. Their main mistake was selling options without buying them back on capital markets to hedge them. This is indeed a managerial choice the consequences of which have to be fully understood and accepted. This is precisely where 'virtual' financial markets teach their most useful lesson. Risk management tools, derivatives, are widely available, which begs the question of whether financial and non-financial corporations should use them. There is no direct answer. However, the question is a strong indication of where to look. A psychoanalyst would call it an introspection work. The corporation has to define what it is good at, its core competence as business strategists would call it. This in turn means that it is able to distinguish, like the Cornish fisherman, the risks that it wants to keep and those that it wants to shift away. Ohio State University Professor of Finance, René Stulz, illustrates this quite nicely with the example of a legendary firm, Harley Davidson (Stulz, 1996). In the late 1970s one might have been tempted to say that Harley Davidson had no foreign currency exposure of any importance. It did not export to Japan and could be perceived as having no yen/dollar exposure. Such a diagnosis would have been wrong. An appreciating US dollar versus the yen could convince Japanese motorcycle producers to export to the United States, thus threatening the competitive position of

Harley Davidson in its own home market. As René Stulz puts it 'if one knows the value drivers of the corporation, one knows enough to be able to identify the risks that affect firm value'. As an information tool, the virtual economy allows the identification and evaluation of risks 'buried' in corporate balance sheets. Having fully quantified the risks they face, managers are then able to concentrate on the firm's true expertise. One could add to this that, because derivatives markets allow a wide range of risks to be traded, they help the firm decipher which are the risks where it has a leading edge. Stulz's lesson works both ways: the identification and improvement of one's own expertise entails a full knowledge of all the risks one faces, and vice versa. For instance, insurance companies should have realised (they have now) that granting options to their policyholders was tantamount to loading interest rate risk into their balance sheets. The insurance company has no competitive edge whatsoever with respect to this risk. As René Stulz notes, it is 'hard to believe that managers for whom the (financial) markets is a part-time activity at best are likely to be able to beat professionals who spend all their time devising investment strategies'. This is, of course, good news for the policyholder to know that he can benefit from interest hedging provisions. He is better off. However, it requires the insurance company to be fully aware of the promises it has made and, in turn, to hedge them properly thanks to the derivatives markets.

Nevertheless, a few recent disasters might tend to undermine this lesson. The staggering losses made on derivatives by companies such as Procter & Gamble, Orange County, Gibson Greetings, Barings and Metallgesellschaft are horror stories liable to dissuade 'responsible' managers from utilising the derivatives tools coined by 'virtual finance'. To use the words of Nobel Laureate and University of Chicago Professor of Economics, Merton H. Miller, 'Just as one can dispel the fear of a child who thinks there is something under his bed by shining a light on the dreaded spot, so can one perhaps calm the public's fears by explaining the real facts of these so-called horror stories' (Miller, 1997).

The case of German firm Metallgesellschaft is very revealing. Metallgesellschaft is a large industrial conglomerate whose activities range from mining to financial services. At the beginning of 1994, the company announced a loss of US$1.3 billion on derivatives positions taken by its US subsidiary Metallgesellschaft Refining and Marketing (hereafter MGRM). At the time, these losses were the largest derivatives-linked losses ever incurred by a single corporation. To avoid the collapse of the group, which had a turnover of US$16 billion and employed 43 000 people, an emergency rescue plan was put in place. This plan involved an injection of US$1.9 billion by the firm's 150 German and international creditor banks. On the announcement of these figures, the press jumped on the affair and claimed that here was another victim of the folly of the derivatives markets. Senior management at the German headquarters climbed on to the bandwagon and claimed that 'speculative oil deals had plunged Metallgesellschaft into the crisis'. A less superficial examination reveals not only that the derivatives-based hedging strategy adopted by the US subsidiary was suitable, but also that the precipitous unwinding of the hedging strategy might well have pushed Metallgesellschaft belly up.

MGRM was engaged in the refining and distribution of petroleum products such as gasoline and heating oil to both large and small customers. Its marketing strategy was rather aggressive and consisted in offering long-term price guarantees (up to 10 years) on oil products to customers. In order to implement this programme and to avoid leaving the firm exposed to hikes in oil prices, MGRM's management decided to carry out a hedging operation based on financial derivatives. Without going into too much detail, its principle was to provide MGRM with a cover against the volatility of oil prices. It involved the purchase of a series of short-term oil and oil products futures contracts and swap contracts whose function was to hedge the fixed price promise made to clients. This promise was valuable to many clients: it gave them oil price visibility by removing oil price volatility and transferring it to MGRM. This made sense indeed because MGRM was better equipped to use futures or swap markets for hedging purposes than most of its clients. When the oil prices started to fall in autumn 1993, MGRM had to face significant and growing funding problems. Indeed, the standard practice in futures markets is to mark-to-market futures contracts on a daily basis; that is, to value their positions at current prices. This forces losers to recognise their losses immediately and to post the required cash (so-called margin calls) with the exchange. This ensures that the market remains solvent. As a result, MGRM was forced to register the pending losses on its futures position and to post additional cash with the clearing house. These margin calls can be painful, but they are a clear indication of the volatile nature of MGRM's oil business. They were also an indication that the other leg of the transaction; that is, MGRM's hedged business, had become more valuable. Unfortunately, this side was less visible than the margin calls. Metallgesellschaft's top management seems to have panicked and overreacted. It decided to unwind; that is, to cancel, the whole futures position. Yet, Nobel Laureate, Merton

H. Miller, argues that the hedging programme was sound and that Metallgesellschaft's hasty decision made the situation worse than it really was. Somehow, Metallgesellschaft decided to shoot the messenger instead of trying to decipher what the message meant.

Likewise, the southeast Asian crisis of 1996 seems to suggest that modern financial markets are causing more harm than anything else. For how can it be explained that South Korea, Indonesia, Malaysia, Thailand, the admired Tigers or Dragons, were swept away in the space of a few weeks? These tigers were symbols not only of growth but also of hard work. Some observers of the Asian miracle had even predicted the emergence of a Pacific pole, which was steadily shifting the centre of gravity of the world economy. This enthusiasm was abruptly dissipated. Within a few chaotic weeks, the dream was shattered. The Tigers had become Paper Tigers. They had become the epicentres of an earthquake, which threatened to rock the whole world economy.

A conspiracy theory gained ground quite rapidly. It seemed impossible that economies that had worked so hard could collapse like a mere house of cards. Malaysia's Prime Minister denounced a conspiracy instigated by powerful interests. Financiers were immediately suspected of having fomented some diabolical plan. MIT Professor of Economics, Rudiger Dornbusch, describes how a rumour quickly spread that New York financiers had one objective in mind: to bring the Asian Tigers to their knees. The almighty capital markets were accused of serving this sinister plan.

Disarray is obviously not conducive to serene thinking. The anger of the Asian political leaders is understandable. For decades, their countries had worked hard to generate growth, which had been so much admired by Western countries. Yet, the fruits of this unremitting toil were about to vanish in the air leaving them petrified. The Asian miracle seemed to have become the Asian nightmare.

None the less, this brutal economic blow does not excuse the flow of inaccuracies and flawed explanations that were disseminated. There was an initial question that few economic observers dared to ask at the time. It seemed incongruous and iconoclastic: was there really an Asian miracle in the first place? Should one have talked about an Asian mirage instead? Clearly, this was not an easy question to ask. However, at the time when Asia was still enjoying economic euphoria, some economists had the guts to ask it. Indeed, the quasi-miraculous nature of the Asian growth begged for an explanation. The ingredients of the Asian growth recipe had to be understood. These same economists were astonished when they discovered that the miracle seemed to have been more like a mirage.

NBER researcher and Professor of Economics, Alwyn Young (1992, 1994) and MIT Professor of Economics, Paul Krugman (1994), were the first to set the cat among the pigeons when they described the Asian Tigers as Paper Tigers. Their argument is quite straightforward. First, it was rather naive to think that the 8% to 10% growth rate of southeast Asian countries was indefinitely sustainable. Falling rates were inevitable and the frenetic rate of investment would have to be lowered. Second, economic growth shall not be judged only in quantitative terms. Its main drivers have to be thoroughly examined. According to Young and Krugman, the Asian Tigers' economic growth, unlike that of Japan after the Second World War, was not linked to productivity gains but, instead, was the result of a massive mobilisation of labour and capital. Krugman describes Asia's growth as Soviet accumulation – end of story! When economists started to look closely at Soviet Union economic growth, they discovered that Khrushchev's famous 'we will bury you' speech to the Western world was predicated on an input-driven policy: more and more people at work and more factories constructed but hardly any efficiency gains. The rest of the story is known. It is very hard to believe the Asian miracle was driving its momentum from the same sources. But, the figures are there. Taking the example of Singapore, Krugman shows that 'the miracle turns out to have been based on perspiration rather than inspiration'. This 'blood and sweat' type of growth has obvious limitations. Once everyone has been put to work, the potential for growth is saturated unless significant gains in productivity can be obtained. Productivity gains were lacking in Asia and, in their absence, the cake could not be made any bigger.

One cannot criticise Young and Krugman for being wise after the event, since their analysis predates the crisis. True, it does not explain the suddenness and severity of the Asian crisis, but it is perhaps surprising that their findings were not given more attention. There are two main reasons for this. The first is that, as part of the inevitable and legitimate academic debate over their work, numerous experts questioned the validity of their approach. The second reason is more subtle: the perverse effects of moral hazard. Despite the quality of Young and Krugman's research and their early warning signals, a lot of economic players found it optimal not to worry. Indeed, why worry when one knows that governmental and International Monetary Fund (IMF) (implicit) guarantees will come to the rescue in case of an emergency? Once again, the 'Monte Carlo' strategy syndrome is at work. The only difference, this time, is that the strategy has been applied on a continental scale!

Yet the macroeconomic indicators of some countries such as Thailand seemed to be exemplary. As MIT's Rudiger Dornbusch has noted, there was nothing really wrong about Thailand: strong growth, negligible inflation, budget surpluses and a comfortable level of savings. Nevertheless, closer examination of the statistics did indeed reveal a blemish: a significant deficit on the current account balance of the Thai balance of payments. But, why would this deficit cause any problems? To fully understand the chain reaction that was actually involved, one or two basic principles and definitions are in order.

The current account balance is a record of the trade in goods, services and of unilateral transfers between a country and the rest of world. By unilateral transfers, one understands payments made abroad, or received from abroad. They may include development aid, and gifts and wages repatriated by foreign workers. In other words, the current account balance measures the country's financial position *vis-à-vis* the rest of the world. A current account deficit means that the country needs funding and has to obtain it by borrowing from international lenders. Conversely, a country with a surplus on its current account balance is in a net lending position *vis-à-vis* the rest of the world. The same holds true for a private corporation. When its business yields negative operating cash flows, it needs extra funding to sustain its development. Internet firms with their 'galactic' burn rates are a good example of such situations. Through the 1990s, South Korea, Indonesia, Malaysia, the Philippines and Thailand recorded significant deficits on their current account balances. Thailand, for example, posted an average deficit of 7.5% of its Gross National Product (GNP). A country confronted with a current account deficit of this size must raise funds from external sources to bridge the gap. It can consider borrowing from domestic or international banks, or else directly on the financial markets. It is important to note that the type of borrowing chosen is not entirely neutral in its effects. The accumulation of highly volatile short-term debt – 'hot money' – may create a high degree of vulnerability that the indebted country cannot ignore. In contrast, foreign direct investment is by definition more stable.

Southeast Asian countries are not the only ones recording a current account deficit. In fact, the majority of developing countries have current account deficits. The financial indicators regularly published by UK magazine *The Economist* document this phenomenon. What is more, this type of deficit is not restricted to developing countries alone. The United States has recorded a current account deficit for quite a long time. As of March 2000, this deficit is around US$300 billion. Besides, this deficit has raised fierce debates in the United States. The primary bone of contention has always been the deficit with Japan. As everyone knows, the American trade deficit with Japan is quite considerable to the extent that the debate around it left the purely economic arena to become a very sensitive political issue. The deficit was a hot topic during the last presidential campaign, and a degree of 'Japanophobia', monitored by powerful and influential circles, spread throughout the United States. The obsession with the trade deficit and the shame of being in a debtor position with a country defeated in the Second World War were powerful ingredients in this anti-Japan campaign. Ex-Under Secretary of the

Department of Commerce Robert Ortner (1990) summarises the situation quite well when he talks about 'Voodoo deficit'.

Yet, there are few legitimate reasons not to worry too much about this American account deficit. It could even be that it is good news for the American economy. The fact is that the Japanese savings rate is one of the highest in the world. These savings, moreover, are not totally absorbed by domestic investment. Investment opportunities must be found outside Japan. The US economy, thanks to its dynamism, is the primary place where these savings are invested. Hence, the American economy finances its growth by attracting foreign savings. A private corporation does just the same thing when it borrows money from banks and capital markets. Obviously, in order to invest in the United States, the Japanese must obtain US dollars and that is exactly what their trade surplus with the United States provides them with. If America does well, the Japanese investment will generate suitable revenues, from exports in particular, which will be used to settle the debt with Japan. Profitable investments have obviously to be chosen. The same holds for a private corporation. A corporation has to create wealth to reward both the shareholders and the lenders for their investments. To make sure that this is indeed the case, monitoring devices have to be put in place. The investment profitability must be monitored, both by an active financial market and by a solid financial intermediation structure – as is the case in the United States. Without such a framework, there is a significant risk that the investment will follow a 'Monte Carlo' strategy pattern.

To put it in a nutshell, the American deficit is a reflection both of the high level of Japanese savings and of the vitality of the American economy. Nobel Laureate and Hoover Institution Fellow, Milton Friedman, was once astonished that this deficit could be viewed as bad news: 'It is a mystery to me why, to take a specific example, it is regarded as a sign of Japanese strength and US weakness that the Japanese find it more attractive to invest in the US than in Japan. Surely it is the reverse – a sign of US strength and Japanese weakness' (Friedman, 1988). All deficits, then, are not bad in themselves. A more important question is whether the country is getting into debt for good or bad reasons. An indebted country can, indeed, be extremely vulnerable both to internal and external shocks. This is especially true if the country has a fragile (or even non-existent) banking system, is handicapped by a massive short-term external debt and if, to add insult to injury, it is affected by corruption and crony capitalism. This is why the sight of impressive skylines sparkling in the night sky should only beguile tourists. Skyscrapers sprouting like mushrooms often conceal foundations made of deficits, blunders and embezzlement.

But how does this digression deepen our understanding of the turbulence that has engulfed southeast Asia? During the 1990s, all the Asian countries accumulated deficits on their current account balance. These deficits were tolerated because the countries' high growth rates, so highly praised, were taken to be a firm guarantee of their ability to repay their growing debt. Their level of investment – up to 40% of Gross Domestic Product (GDP) – was much higher than their level of savings. The domestic euphoria entailed an increase in private consumption, thereby lowering the level of domestic savings. The current account balance deficits widened. This would not have been a problem if the investments had been wise ones. Actually, the opposite was true. People started to talk about over-investment in dubious industrial sectors – such as low-tech semiconductors in South Korea – and in real estate. Because of an over-capacity in the property sector, the value of real estate investments plummeted in 1996–1997. Businesses and individuals defaulted on mortgage loan repayments as well as the banks, which had imprudently lent them money. These same banks were unable to repay their international claim-holders. An exacerbating factor was that most of the loans were denominated in domestic currencies, whereas the banks' own borrowings were mostly in US dollars. These domestic banks had not seen the need to hedge their financial risks – relating to exchange and interest rates – primarily because of the closeness, not to say intimacy, of their relationships with their respective national governments. After all, all they were doing was implementing on a massive scale the good old 'Monte Carlo' strategy. Why bother hedging against risks when that is what the State's guarantee is implicitly providing? The fall of the domestic currencies following the confidence crisis only added insult to injury. Risks compounded and dragged the countries down.

Why was this mismanagement tolerated for so long, in particular by the international lenders who are normally so shrewd? The Monte Carlo strategy was once again at work. It was harmful because it was applied in the context of fragile financial systems. The domestic institutions did not have a large equity base. As a result, they had nothing much to lose in placing bets. This gambling behaviour went wild because a lot of financial institutions were state-owned, or indirectly controlled by the local government. Depositors and lenders did not worry much because of the explicit or implicit guarantees given by the government or the IMF. In the same way, international investors were relying upon the IMF to bail them out in the case of an emergency. Steve Hanke, Professor of Applied Economics at the Johns Hopkins University does not mince his words: 'The IMF ultimately goes to the rescue of those who do not deserve it ... In other words, there are no penalties for wrong doing.'

The conclusion to be drawn from the Asian crisis is clear. The situation is aptly summarised by the comments of the Harvard University Professor of Economics and Under Secretary of Treasury, Lawrence Summers: 'The Asian crisis is a reflection of non-market finance, the allocation of capital on bases other than where it will find its highest return.' Whether the conspiracy theorists like it or not, the crisis was not linked to some kind of financial hypertrophy but rather to a shortage of finance. Asia allowed Gresham's law[2] to take the lead: bad finance drove out good finance.

Irony or mere coincidence? The 1998 Russian crisis, the difficulties of the Brazilian economy and the explosion of volatility in the financial markets in the last quarter of 1998 seem to invalidate the diagnosis drawn from the Asian debacle. Bank failures, crazy rumours, falling prices, 'flight to quality', redundancies in the City and on Wall Street – all the actors seemed to have come together for the first and perhaps the last performance of a bad play. On top of this, some unexpected stars appeared in the scenario. Robert C. Merton and Myron Scholes, who shared the Nobel Prize for Economics in 1997, were caught up in the sensational near-collapse of the Long-Term Capital Management (LTCM) hedge fund, which they had created

---

[2] After Sir Thomas Gresham, English merchant, financier and founder of the Royal Exchange. Gresham's law says that 'bad money drives out good money'.

some three years earlier together with a handful of high-flying financiers. Alan Greenspan, the all-powerful chairman of the Federal Reserve, was forced to play Superman and come to the rescue of the markets by introducing surprise cuts in interest rates.

All this was enough to prompt *Le Monde Diplomatique*, a French intelligentsia newspaper, in November 1998, to denounce the rudderless ship of finance and to call once again for a firm control of financial markets. French sociologist, Ignacio Ramonet, and *Le Monde Diplomatique*'s editorial team published that month a special issue on 'the anatomy of the financial crisis'. This issue echoed the creation, a few months earlier, of an international organisation (inspired by the Tobin tax on capital market transactions), ATTAC, the Association pour une Taxation des Transactions Financières pour l'Aide aux Citoyens. This awkwardly named organisation declared its ambitious objective: 'working together to regain the control of the future of our world'. The monthly French magazine *Alternatives Economiques* headlined its October 1998 issue: 'Financial markets: the threat'. It contained two articles, entitled 'How finance has become uncontrollable' and 'World casino seeks regulator'. Susan Strange, Professor of Economics at the University of Warwick, condemned international finance for being 'completely irrational'. At around the same time, French President Chirac also joined the fray, and urged the implementation of a 'Highway Code' for financial flows.

Again, both speculators and the financial markets were pilloried. This outright condemnation is no surprise, of course. But, this time, markets' detractors were convinced that they now possessed evidence which they previously lacked. Admittedly, the opportunity seems too beautiful to be true: two Nobel Laureates caught red-handed. *The Economist*, the weekly UK magazine, added a note of humour when it announced the 1998 Nobel Prize Laureate, Cambridge University economist, Amartya Sen. According to the magazine, the Swedish Academy had, for once, decided to award its prize to an economist who had spent his whole life working out how to dismantle the mechanisms of poverty in order to enrich the world's poorest people. What a contrast, *The Economist* commented, with the previous year, when the Academy had awarded its highest distinction to two economists who were so keen to impoverish a large number of rich people!

Joking apart, this condemnation of the financial markets cannot simply be shrugged off. In fact, the argument is suspect. Speculation and its foot soldiers, the hedge funds, are selected as special targets. Speculative operations, financial leverage, and the pernicious derivatives are the alarming ingredients entrusted to sorcerers' apprentices who do not care about the disastrous consequences of their actions. Once again, superficial analysis prevails. Yet, the pressing need is to understand, in order to be able to explain. In this respect, it is not a bad idea to look at what Joseph Proudhon, French socialist and Karl Marx's son-in-law, thought of speculation. At the beginning of the Second Empire, Proudhon published a pamphlet entitled 'Manual for speculators on the stock exchange'. This work has more than one lesson for us. In it, Proudhon provides one of the best definitions of speculation:

Speculation is no more than an intellectual notion encompassing the different processes through which work, credit, transport and trade can be involved in production. It is speculation which seeks and discovers what we might call the wealth opportunities, which invents the most economical means for procuring wealth, and which multiplies it, whether by new methods or by combinations of credit, transport, capital and trade, or by the creation of new needs, or even by the dissemination and ceaseless movement of fortunes.

Proudhon does not deny the difficulty of understanding and accepting speculation, and he stresses its double-edged nature when he compares it simultaneously to a 'spirit of liberty' and to a 'Satan reiterating his refusal to obey'. This arrogant quest for liberty cannot fail to annoy governments which view it as a permanent denial of their prerogatives. Nor can it fail to disturb those who express regret for the good old days when the economy was more watertight.

Yet, there is a kind of schizophrenia in the criticisms about capital markets, such as Montesquieu denounced in his famous *Lettres Persanes* (Montesquieu, 1721). Usbek the Persian meets a man who is in the depths of despair. His tenant farmers have stopped paying him their rent. His buildings are falling apart and he is overwhelmed by taxes. He begins to regret not having invested his fortune in stocks and shares. Usbek continues on his way and meets another man, also in deep despair. This man's Mississippi shares have tumbled and he regrets not having invested in land, which would always be there. The same old debate, then, which the turmoil of markets only serves to rekindle. Unfortunately, the critics of capital markets see only one possible outcome to this debate: a tightening up of the regulations. In their opinion, some sand needs to be sprinkled into the markets' wheels, to give more control over the direction and speed of international flows of capital. This is a reactionary attitude, and one that displays a complete lack of understanding of the anatomy and purpose of modern financial markets. Regulation ought to be constantly re-inventing itself and not tightening up in a self-protective reaction which can only cause widespread harm. The third parable in this book underlines the great importance of viewing the modern economy in functional terms. Imposing restrictions on financiers will not help at all; it will end up reducing risk reallocation opportunities and penalise society as a whole. After all, economic life is made of ups and downs that have to be actively managed.

The famous French columnist and academician of the 1930s, Jacques Bainville (1937), displayed an extraordinarily clear under-standing of this point in his contribution to the newspaper *Le Capital* on 13 February, 1936, when he wrote:

Capitalism is not in the process of 'falling apart', because it has always been falling apart. It is made up of a series of destructions and constructions.... There is also an art not only in being rich but in being a capitalist, an art which consists in knowing above all that wealth is not eternal, that it is fragile and that it is continually re-forming itself, in new circumstances, and rarely in the same hands.

This last point is fundamental. Alan Greenspan, chairman of the Federal Reserve, was criticised for mixing the public with the private when he put all his weight behind resolving the LTCM hedge fund crisis. This was an insult to his intelligence, though. At no point was public money used to compensate LTCM's losses. The affair was settled between private partners who assumed sole responsibility for providing the additional funds required to rescue the fund and bring it gradually back to the surface (see Dunbar, 1999).

The markets' detractors use this perceived ambiguity a lot, by muddling social losses (that is, the loss of wealth suffered by society as a whole) and private losses. Losses on the derivatives markets (futures and options) are denounced. Money is wasted and definitely lost to society. This is simply not true. These losses are purely private losses that compensate each other, leaving society's total wealth intact. Indeed, a loss on a derivatives contract means by definition that there is a symmetrical gain in another part of the economy. What would be the use of derivative products if they were not designed specifically as wealth transfer vehicles? For, as Jacques Bainville fully understood, wealth is volatile: 'It is nice to hear abuse hurled at "acquired wealth" when one has just seen how disappointing and how fragile it is!'

Utilisation of the virtual economy is too often not understood by many decision-makers. Of course, the astounding pace of growth of derivatives markets is relatively recent. Few senior managers have so far had the opportunity to really study these instruments and the possibilities that they open up. Unfortunately, more cases like that of Metallgesellschaft will occur in the future. A new generation well versed in these new techniques is needed to take over the baton. Indeed, the calculations that have to be made, and the information technology required to design proper financial instruments, are becoming increasingly sophisticated. As Peter Bernstein (1993) says, the manager is no longer 'the witch doctor trying to cure a patient by jumping up and down until the patient is healed just by the passage of time, and the witch doctor can then take the credit for the cure'.

Imagine a passenger at Heathrow airport ready to leave for New York. He has the choice between two different aircraft. The first emerged from the Airbus factory, after thousands of hours of design, calculations on high-powered computers, and test flights. The second is just like the first, in appearance at least. The only difference is the fact that it was designed on a portable personal computer. The passenger chooses the sophisticated aircraft without any hesitation. There is no reason to believe that the same thing does not occur in finance. Didier Dacunha-Castelle (1996) quite rightly points out that 'arming oneself against adversity does have a price, and for one thousand seven hundred years, this price has been calculated case by case, on the basis of experience and without any precise rules'. He underlines the importance of the emergence of the mathematical law of large numbers in the development of many human activities. Further on, he states that:

the notions of equilibrium, of arbitrage in the markets, of equity-hedging strategies, all familiar in the world of finance, can be expressed in clear and elegant mathematical terms within a framework of probability theory.... It seems logical, then, that finance should adopt this mathematical type of language permanently – not just as a passing fad – and that the arithmetic of probability should be taught in business schools.

It is to be hoped that greater familiarity with the quantitative techniques of the virtual economy will open the eyes of those who are tempted to dole out irresponsible promises. University of California at Berkeley Professor of Sociology, Ibrahim Warde, misses the point when, talking about the use of mathematics in economics, he claims that 'as formerly in the case of Latin, mathematics is now needed to underpin the authority of the pundits' (Warde, 1995). On what grounds can one reasonably expect that a complex financial contract solving a complex real-world issue does not deserve the same thorough scientific treatment as an aeroplane wing or a microprocessor? Only ignorance would suggest such an idea.

The virtual economy, after all, only mirrors the tyranny of the real economy. It is there precisely to avoid situations where promises are binding only on those who receive them. Unfortunately, there is often a great temptation to blame the mirror – even to break it – because of the image that it reflects. The mirror is in no way responsible for that image, and, actually, should be commended for revealing it. The virtual economy should no longer be blamed for the breaking of very real promises. Virtual economy and failed promises do not go well together – on the contrary! Red Sea pearl-fishers were not victims of toxic financial derivatives. The opposite is true. They eventually lost their share because a banker had incentives not to use hedging devices but to go for broke. The same was true in Asia and in Russia. Geronimo learnt this lesson at his own and his people's expense. When incentives are not properly aligned, when regulators mess up the functioning of markets, the shadows of the Red Sea banker and of the 'Tucson clique' loom up and the worst is to be feared.

Still, despite having been betrayed so many times by so many Tribolets, Geronimo never reneged on his word. During the summer of 1904, S.M. Barrett, Chief Inspector of Education in Lawton, Oklahoma, met him. He had been taken prisoner and deported far from his native Arizona to Fort Sill, where he ended his days growing watermelons. Despite the Apache chief's very understandable mistrust of a paleface, Barrett managed to create ties of friendship with him and even persuaded him to tell him the story of his life. He spent whole days with Geronimo and another Indian, Asa Daklugie, who acted as interpreter. The old chief was very punctilious. He had a keen sense of honour that impressed Barrett. One day in January 1906, Barrett was waiting for Geronimo to come to his office. Asa Daklugie arrived on his own, announcing that the old chief was very ill, suffering from a fever, and that it would be better to arrange another date for the meeting. Asa Daklugie had scarcely apologised on Geronimo's behalf when they saw, through the window, a little dot on the horizon, rapidly approaching. Barrett recognised the figure of the aged chief on his horse. He jumped to the ground and entered, muttering hoarsely: 'I promised to come. Here I am'. Barrett was embarrassed and told Geronimo that it would have been better for him to have rested. Geronimo said nothing, remounted his pony and went out into the cold, blustery wind. Despite his poor health, he had, once again, like the pearl-fishers of the Red Sea and unlike the 'Monte Carlo' banker, kept his promise.

THE PARABLE OF THE GENOESE
MERCHANT AND THE MOLECULE

Mother Nature's quirks have always been a threat to mankind. In ancient times, peasants whose sole means of subsistence lay in agriculture would seek to ward off these perils by visiting their simple places of worship and enlisting the assistance of their benevolent saints and gods. In Burgundy, a French province famous for its magnificent wines, wine growers would pray to Saint Medard and Sainte Barbe for clement weather. Indeed, Saint Medard was venerated on the grounds of his ability to make rain, while Sainte Barbe's ability to chase away lightning is legendary. However, this celestial form of coverage was usually supplemented with some down-to-earth form of hedging. For instance, sea navigators would not only pray to Saint Guenole, but would also prudently arrange some contracts to mitigate their exposure to sea perils.

Indeed, marine navigation has always been a hazardous venture and this was one of the primary risks faced by medieval businessmen. As French historian Jean Favier (1987) writes, 'Travel by sea was definitely the foremost trade risk'. The list of dangers was endless: tempests could destroy a merchant's efforts and capital; entire vessels, along with their precious cargoes, could be swallowed by surging currents; navigators relied solely on astral signposts and were even denied these when the weather turned; captains and crewmates could only count on their experience and courage. And even when the weather was calm, there was always the danger from greedy buccaneers and pirates who preyed on merchant shipping, stealing cargo and selling crew members into slavery – if they were lucky. This concentration of risks upon a single focus, the ship, made sea travel a life-threatening business and should in itself have led to a slowdown in the growth of trade.

Yet, marine trade continued to grow and to link ever more remote geographical points as merchants began to use larger vessels, capable of sailing farther from the safety of coastlines. Escorts were offered to discourage attack but, while this was safer, it also cost money, thus raising the cost of trade. In Venice, for example, merchants had a clear choice: they could either use private ships without escort and take their chances or, for an additional fee, they could sail under the protection of official vessels. The cost rendered the choice a difficult one. There was no doubt that armed fleets discouraged the boldest of pirates, but their cost was prohibitive and substantially eroded profits. It was far cheaper to sail without protection, provided the ship actually reached its destination! Shipowners in Marseilles dealt with this dilemma by inventing the system of the crown to spread the risks over several merchants. In 1387, 14 merchants from Marseilles formed a crown to operate a ship at a total cost of 2000 florins, with every participant contributing from 30 to 200 florins (see Favier, 1991). While this reduced individual jeopardy, the risk was not entirely transferred and some improvements were necessary.

According to Jean Favier, a Genoese merchant named Benedetto Zaccaria had to ship 30 tons of alum in 1298, from Aigues Mortes to Bruges, where he had located a buyer. Zaccaria was aware of the contingencies. With the help of two Genoese financiers, Baliano Grilli and Enrico Suppa, he struck an interesting deal through a contract which was designed to shift the risk away from Zaccaria's business. This is how it worked: Zaccaria sold the alum to Suppa and Grilli on the spot at an agreed price. The alum was then loaded on a vessel that would head for Bruges. Provided the vessel reached Bruges safely, Zaccaria was committed to repurchase the alum from Suppa and Grilli, after which he would then sell it to his local client. Naturally, the repurchase price was much higher than the price of the initial spot transaction. If things went wrong, say, due to a storm and the alum was lost during the voyage, Zaccaria would not owe anything to Suppa and Grilli. In other words, Suppa and Grilli granted Zaccaria an option to default on the repurchase transaction. A modern economist would say that the three Genoese businessmen had come up with a non-linear risk-sharing rule. Viewed from Zaccaria's point of view, the risk-sharing rule is convex: he was (i.e. owned) long an option to default. Moreover, the transaction offered the considerable advantage of being accepted by such scholars as Saint Thomas, who condemned the very notion of interest rates. The transaction between Zaccaria, Suppa and Grilli was more subtle, since it involved only sales and repurchase operations. The theological concept of *damnum emergens* prevailed: there was a physical risk, for which it was deemed legitimate to compensate. Thus, two problems were solved simultaneously in a single structure. By acquiring the option, Zaccaria had not abandoned his role as a merchant. On the contrary, the transfer of an exogenous risk to people who felt capable of underwriting it enabled him to focus better on his business. The physical and ecclesiastical bogies were duly dealt with. Suppa and Grilli negotiated an attractive repurchase price and underwrote Zaccaria's physical marine risk without incurring the wrath of the ecclesiastics.

But can we tell more about Suppa and Grilli? Were they insurers, bankers or derivatives traders? Did Zaccaria subscribe to an insurance policy? Did he strike an investment banking deal or purely a capital market transaction? Bankers will obviously claim the paternity of the deal since, after all, Zaccaria had paid no up-front (insurance) premium to Suppa and Grilli. Insurers would definitely dismiss this as nonsense, claiming that Suppa and Grilli had acted as an insurance company since they agreed to underwrite the entire burden of the risk (see Gusten, 1996). In other words, if one were to believe them, Zaccaria signed an insurance contract with Suppa and Grilli. Interestingly enough, though, Zaccaria had no intention of bracketing himself as an insured party or as a bank client. He could not care less! What mattered to him was to be relieved from a risk that was outside his talent and control.

Yet, this answer does not satisfy either insurers or bankers. Twenty-first century insurers still dislike being compared to bankers and the converse is probably true. In other words, if Suppa and Grilli were insurers, they could not also be bankers, and vice versa. That said, modern consumers also draw a similar line of distinction between banks and insurance companies. This is hardly surprising. Banks and insurance companies are subject to different regulations and are governed by different supervisory authorities (with the recent exception of the United Kingdom). Both have their own industry organisations. For consumers, the regulations covering bank loans are different from those regulating insurance contracts. If they were living in the twenty-first century, Enrico Suppa and Baliano Grilli would have to opt for a precise 'institutional status', while Benedetto Zaccaria would have had to choose whether to be a bank client or a policyholder.

Obviously, many factors have contributed to this differentiation between banks and insurance companies. Insurers have energetically pleaded their case and advocated the unique nature of their business. Their stance is traditionally fuelled by three key arguments, namely the so-called 'inversion' of the insurance production cycle, the notion of liability risk-taking and the duration of their liabilities.

The first argument, which occurs quite frequently in major actuarial sciences and insurance management textbooks, states that the insurance production cycle is unique. The sale price of insurance (i.e. the premium) must be determined before its true cost price (its cost in the event of claims) is known. An insurance company does not know whether or not a loss will occur. At best, it must rely on the law of large numbers by grouping a large cohort of policyholders within the same insurance portfolio. Insurance pricing therefore requires a very special expertise and that is the job of the 'rocket scientists' of insurance who go by the name of actuaries. According to the second argument, an insurance company selling an insurance contract accepts a contingent commitment that adds to its liabilities. Conversely, a bank granting a real estate or commercial mortgage loan holds a claim that is added to its assets. The insurance company is a debtor to its client. Writing an insurance contract is tantamount to issuing a promise. The third argument focuses on the length of commitments accepted by insurance companies, especially life insurance companies. Annuity payments span a significant length of time and the servicing period can be far longer than expected and priced due to the risk of longevity.

These arguments tend to suggest that matters have changed a great deal since the thirteenth century. Indeed, at first sight, it may seem that insurance companies have become a unique breed, a world apart from banks. However, this distinction is erroneous, since banking and insurance are not really dissimilar activities. Benedetto Zaccaria knew this a long time ago!

The first argument can be negated by two simple examples. Options markets quote call and put option prices – even though option buyers and sellers do not know in advance whether or not their options will be exercised. In the case of mortgages, banks grant prepayment options and must therefore price in a provision that may, or may not, be used by the client. Suppa and Grilli were in the same situation. They could not foretell whether Zaccaria would call on them to bail him out of a disaster, or whether he would complete his voyage safely. In case of a loss at sea, or an act of piracy, Zaccaria would exercise his default right. In other words, although insurers do not actually use the word 'option', selling an insurance contract is nevertheless tantamount to selling an option contract. The policy-holder pays a premium to the insurer for the right to transfer his or her loss to the insurance company. It is, therefore, clear that an insurance contract and an option functionally provide the same service. The holder of a put option has the guarantee that the value of the asset at risk is protected by the put. Car insurance is a good example: when a loss exceeds the insurance deductible (if any), a policyholder will exercise his or her right to indemnification. The difference between the value of the loss and the deductible will thus be the perceived net receipt. By contrast, if the loss is less than the deductible, then there will be no net receipt and the loss will be effectively paid for by the policyholder. The deductible plays the same role as the strike price in an option contract. Hence, the boundaries between insurance and derivatives are more and more blurred. The recent development of so-called catastrophe bonds offers another good example. These bonds are characterised by the fact that their coupons and/or their principal are exposed to the occurrence of natural catastrophes. Their potential yield is usually high in order to compensate the lender for the possible loss of the coupons and/principal to which he or she is entitled. In other words, the lender acts as if he or she were an insurance company by insuring the borrower against damage caused by natural catastrophes. In the case of a claim, the borrower reimburses nothing and can therefore use the funds not reimbursed to pay for his or her losses. For example, Winterthur, the Swiss insurance company, recently floated a bond in order to hedge itself against hail risk, since heavy hailstones can result in significant vehicle body damage. Traditionally, insurance companies cede part of their risks to reinsurance companies. However, in this case, Winterthur has chosen an alternative institutional arrangement through the transfer of the hailstone risk to the financial market by means of an instrument that bears a strong resemblance to the solution used several centuries ago by the Genoese merchant, Benedetto Zaccaria. USAA, a mutual insurance company based in San Antonio, Texas, has done the same to hedge its hurricane risk exposure. USAA is a mutual which was created to provide insurance to retired US army officers. But, guess where these officers retire. Mostly to Florida, a geographical area that is sunny but also exposed to hurricanes. USAA then decided to diversify the ways by which it was covering the resulting catastrophic exposure. It now utilises not only the reinsurance market but also the capital market. By doing so it is in a better position to provide adequate cover to its retired clients even though Florida is sometimes closer to hell than heaven! The opportunity to invest in these bonds is also good news for investors. It is a way of improving the diversification of their asset portfolios. Indeed, it is reasonable to assume that hurricanes in Florida are not correlated with, say, the S&P 500 equity index. In other words, hurricanes do not cause the stock exchange to go up or down and vice versa.

The second argument is also quite easy to quash. Bank deposits can be viewed as providing liquidity insurance. A deposit-holder knows that, in the case of unexpected liquidity needs, he or she can cash in his or her deposit, either totally or in part. The analogy with insurance in this case is even stronger: due to the law of large numbers, not everyone is expected to run and withdraw deposits at the same instant. This same notion of risk mutualisation lies precisely at the heart of the insurance industry. To support this counter-argument further, one can point to the existence of indexed Certificates of Deposits (CDs). Banks offer CDs, the return on which comprises a fixed component plus a variable component which is pegged to a specific index. This index can be, say, an equity index. By issuing such deposits, banks are indeed taking liability risks, since they guarantee a floor and also provide a potential bonus. What matters to the consumer is to be able to choose among the largest set opportunities and to be delivered the proper product or service. Lehman Brothers' Head of European Fixed Income Research, Jamil Baz, has his own unique way to describe this process. He likes to compare Wall Street to the pharmaceutical industry. According to him, financial institutions are nothing but pharmaceutical giants engaged in a fierce and endless competition towards the next path-breaking molecule. This molecule will help to produce new drugs (read financial instruments or services) capable of curing the pains and diseases (read risk exposures) of Main

Street (read corporations, investors, individuals). The process starts in 'Wall Street labs' where so-called 'rocket scientists' try to provide the solutions so badly needed by the agents actively involved (or who want to be) in the growth of our economies. In the end, what matters to us is the solution, not so much the institution that has produced it.

The third argument can also be countered effectively. Life insurance companies insist quite often on the long maturity of their liabilities. This long-term view stems from the actuarial dimension of insurance liabilities, a typical example being the life annuity that is paid until death, which may occur very late on. Until recently, as stressed by Wright (1991), 'portfolio philosophy in the life insurance business was centered on the matching of assets and liabilities…. The traditional practices of buying long-term bonds and mortgages and holding them to maturity were based on the long duration of insurance liabilities'. Wright hastens to add that today 'a rethinking of the duration of these (insurance) products is essential'. This rethinking is not only urged by the redesign of life insurance policies themselves, but also by the pressure of competition. Insurance agents bring considerable pressure on companies' headquarters to set initial rates high enough to match or surpass competition and to keep them high, even though interest rates may have fallen. These interwoven effects challenge the long-term view of insurance liabilities. The duration, in other words the interest rate risk exposure of insurance liabilities, is not merely a matter of mortality table analysis and proper discounting. It is also significantly affected by the shape of the contractual liability cash flows. Since insurance liabilities are not (yet) traded, and as accounting practices tend to distort the cash flow picture, this important point is not always clearly understood. Many insurance

87

companies continue to manage their liabilities using a long-term time frame, when they should generally be aiming at a much shorter time frame. The company has no alternative but to invest the premiums paid by its clients in assets which have a duration similar to those of its liabilities. Any other investment strategy would expose the insurance company to significant risks. The promises made to policy-holders must be kept, and the insurance company's investment portfolio is the instrument by which these commitments can be met. An investment in financial assets with too long a maturity compared with the company's liabilities would produce a significant risk discrepancy between assets and liabilities. The company could experience losses, and even bankruptcy, as a result.

Any loss is obviously bad news for the shareholders, because it means that the value of their piece of ownership falls. In simple terms, a shareholder is not there to gamble on the future path of purely random financial variables. A person who would have taken a piece of ownership in Benedetto Zaccaria's business would not have done so with the aim of placing bets on Zaccaria's ability to forecast tempests or the absence of pirates. He or she would have done so because of the ability of Zaccaria to identify clients, even in remote places. That is where Zaccaria added value. Likewise, a shareholder does not invest in a bank, or an insurance company, or any other kind of enterprise, in order to gamble on the fluctuations in interest rates or exchange rates. And, as everyone knows, bets do not always pay off. An investor who wants to gamble on interest rates can do it on his or her own: he or she can buy bonds or derivatives. Investors have a direct access to the various assets quoted on the financial market. What they are looking for is what equity analysts call 'pure plays'. They want to understand what they invest in. It would be rather odd if the fate of banks or insurance companies was no longer in the hands of their managers, but solely or primarily driven by the behaviour of interest rates or exchange rates! Unfortunately, this may happen.

For instance, as reported by Cravath, Swaine & Moore law firm partner, Daniel P. Cunningham (see Smithson and Smith, 1995), the shareholders of personal computer manufacturer Compaq sued the company's management for failing to hedge against exchange rate risk. This risk is pretty significant since more than half of Compaq's sales are non-US. Their argument was simple: holding shares in Compaq should not be tantamount to a speculation on the dollar, the French franc or the Italian lira. Or, at least, shareholders should be kept informed about the risks they may face. It begs also the question of 'the duty to hedge'. In any case, Compaq should have explained what it was doing and why.

At the end of the 1970s a similar failure drove Laker Airlines into bankruptcy. Sir Freddie Laker had invented a very successful concept called Skytrain: flying one of Sir Freddie's planes was as convenient as taking a train. His airline served the London to New York route at unbeatably low fares. The service was so popular that Laker Airlines was unable to meet demand. In order to be able to sustain its growth, Laker Airlines acquired five more DC-10s, through a lease contract. At the time, the dollar was weak. The airline's revenues were mainly in sterling while the lease payments were in US dollars. In 1981 the dollar recovered. Laker Airlines was unable to cope with the new currency situation; indeed, it had not hedged its currency risk exposure. The rise in the dollar was followed by a drop in the number of UK passengers. Despite its undeniable commercial success, Laker Airlines disappeared from the corporate scene. Sir Freddie Laker should have concentrated on running a successful airline, which he was good at. The proper financial derivatives should have been used and we all could have benefited from cheap airline tickets at a time when air travel was expensive. For almost identical reasons, Pan Am, a well established airline, had to pull down the shutters.

Again, the shareholder who wants to experience the thrill of betting on future exchange rates or on interest rate movements can quite easily do it by himself or herself. He or she does not need Compaq or Laker Airlines to do it on his or her behalf. By the same token, insurance companies and banks should not focus on their respective differences in the hope of protecting some kind of 'chasse gardée'. As we have seen, this does not make any sense. Worse, this does not do any good to their clients. Enrico Suppa and Baliano Grilli took a very pragmatic stance in that respect: they wanted Benedetto Zaccaria to be better off. Zaccaria was primarily interested in transferring his risk to outside players and, in 1298, he chose a hybrid solution that could have been engineered by an insurer, a speculator, a banker or a combination of the three. The key question is therefore not whether there is a 'genetic' difference between insurance companies and banks, but whether Zaccaria and all of us can be better off. Fortunately, the answer is positive. A large spectrum of solutions is available thanks to the fascinating development of financial markets. This makes it possible to select the optimum institution for the function that needs to be fulfilled and it is a blessing that modern capital markets in the 'virtual economy' provide effective tools which can address an ever-increasing array of risks faced by those operating in the 'real economy'. They empower individuals and institutions by enabling them to cherry-pick the risks that they want to retain and shift those that they dislike. That is, capital markets reduce the opaqueness of the real economy. No corporation should be allowed to blame its misfortunes on, say, the US dollar or bad weather. Either the corporation adds true value and should hedge itself to preserve this added value, or it uses the US dollar as a smokescreen to hide corporate incompetence. And, as Roger Fauroux, ex-CEO of Saint Gobain and former French Minister of Finance, is used to saying, 'a corporation that does not add value is stealing wealth from the society as a whole'. Or, as Nick Mooney, Head of European weather risk management at Enron has it, 'Buy the weather you want for your business!'. One could add: 'And, you have no excuse not to do so or, at least, not to give it serious consideration!'

This argument obviously applies to both banks and insurance companies. To maintain market share, they have to show their clients that the services and products they provide are useful. This is not always easy to prove, however. And, financial institutions may often fall under the impression that capital markets have only one objective in mind, that of erasing them from the map. For instance, in the United States, commercial banks have gradually been driven out of the mortgage loan market. Much of their mortgage business has been swallowed up by financial market operators and specialist investment banks. Today, mortgages are tradable on a buoyant mortgage-backed securities market. In essence, the financing of mortgages has broken free from its traditional master and has become a 'free agent'. This is the process known as securitisation. Its scope now includes car loans, credit card loans, music rights. UK rock star David Bowie has recently used it to securitise his music rights. The bonds whose cash flows are backed by his future music rights have been nicknamed the 'Bowie bonds'. Needless to say, David Bowie can enjoy an even better life! Investors have access to a new breed of bonds and Bowie's banker is no longer his only funding device. As stressed by University of California at Berkeley Professor of Real Estate, Robert Edelstein, and Jean-Michel Paul (1998) 'securitisation allows for banks to immediately sell large parts of their portfolio on the market'. It enables them to separate 'physically and economically – the financing and the retailing of large parts of banking activity'. As individuals and consumers, we end up better off because we deal with financial institutions that are more efficient in delivering the products and services we need and want. In the same vein, Edelstein and Paul note that 'this extraordinary capacity to finance not on past wealth but on the present value of future anticipated cash flows is at the core of America's dynamic approach to wealth creation.'

The virtual financial economy holds significant opportunities for anyone with genuine expertise. For instance, a few years ago, it was hard to imagine that anyone could diversify his or her expertise without running the risk of losing it. The example of fund managers is a very telling one. Every day, fund managers engage in a ceaseless quest for that Holy Grail of finance: maximum yield at minimum risk! They are also engaged in a quest for size. Recent mega-mergers, such as UBS–SBC, Allianz–Pimco or AXA–UAP, have created mega-fund managers with assets under management of well above US$500 billion. The size does decrease management costs thanks to economies of scale but, providing added value to the investors has also to be on the agenda. For years, Switzerland has enjoyed a solid reputation in the private banking market but, today, this market has raised a lot of appetite. New competition has emerged, but this is not solely attributable to the newly discovered fragility in the traditional virtue of Swiss confidentiality. There is more to it than that. Today, any US fund manager who specialises in US corporate bonds and swaps the performance of a US corporate bond index against a Swiss equity index becomes a formidable competitor for the Swiss private banker since, by using such a swap, the US manager can turn a US corporate bond portfolio into a Swiss equity portfolio. Indeed, the following sequence of events, albeit invented, could serve as another useful example of the opportunities available in the virtual economy. A client wants a highly talented corporate bond manager to invest SWF100 million in the Swiss equity market. The manager could decline the business by virtue of the fact that he is not an equity manager, but he cleverly devises a work-round. He invests the sum in one of his managed corporate bond portfolios and simultaneously swaps the performance of a corporate benchmark index against the Swiss equity index. Thanks to this exchange, the real bond portfolio has become a virtual Swiss equity portfolio. Although its physical structure has not changed, its cash flows walk and talk now like Swiss equity cash flows. Let us suppose, in this example, that the corporate benchmark index exhibits an 11% return, while the Swiss equity index shows a 12% return. Meanwhile, as a direct result of his genuine expertise, the bond manager has outperformed the corporate bond benchmark by 1% (after deducting his fees). But what does this mean for the Swiss client? He receives a return equal to 12% + (13% − 11%), i.e. 14%. Although the corporate bond manager knows nothing about equity and, maybe, even less about the Swiss market, the magic of the swap enables him to export his know-how without leaving home!

The client is better off: he can enjoy the best of two worlds. His or her set of investment opportunities has expanded.

Competition continues to mushroom, and it can sprout from anywhere. Banks, insurance companies and financial intermediaries are therefore now facing significant challenges and, to survive and prosper, they must face up to the vexed question of how to identify and signal their value-added contribution and to discover how it can be exported and improved. According to an old saying, someone who is good at everything is good at nothing. But to be good at anything, one has to be good at something! In a sense, modern finance resembles Proteus, the Greek god of the sea who could change form at will.

Thanks to virtual derivatives engineering, all market-players, whoever they are and wherever they may be, have the opportunity to express their talent or to be delivered the specific products or services they desire. Of course, this freedom naturally leads to an ever-increasing variety of product and, if there is one tyrannical aspect of virtual derivatives finance, then this where it lies. Due to the blossoming range of modern financial instruments, the virtual economy is constantly putting the real economy to some kind of litmus test. By removing risks and redistributing them to proper hands, it lifts the opaque veil that masks true talents. But, it reveals also the absence of added value which may have been conveniently hiding behind the risk fabric. Today, new versions of Zaccaria's seminal insight are at the origin of renewed wealth opportunities. They may even concern areas where they are not expected in the first place.

For example, what more resembles a molecule of methane than another molecule of methane? Its structure is immutable: one atom of carbon and four atoms of hydrogen. As Harvard University Professor of Finance, Peter Tufano (1996), points out, the fact that it is sold by, say, Enron Capital and Trade Resources does not change anything. Customers buy molecules of methane from Enron in the form, say, of heating gas to heat their houses. A *priori*, there is nothing in itself to distinguish the Enron molecule from another molecule, apart from its price, of course. But, Enron Capital and Trade Resources' Chief Executive Officer, Jeffrey K. Skilling, does not share this view (see Tufano, 1996): 'Selling natural gas is getting to be a real business, like selling washing machines. We are taking the simplest commodity there is, a methane molecule, and we are packaging it and delivering it under a brand name, the same way General Electric does.'

A statement of this kind is no surprise, coming from a modern businessman. Any entrepreneur would certainly agree with it. Nevertheless, a closer investigation of Enron's business move is necessary. Enron's managers were clever enough to realise that consumers of natural gas had two main concerns. The first is obvious: that it is delivered when needed. The second is just as important: winters, say, in Chicago and in Canada are harsh. Indeed, Tufano emphasises that 'by 1990... natural gas prices were more volatile than oil prices and, on occasion, four times as volatile as the Standard & Poor's 500 equity index'. A hard winter can turn into a nightmare with gas bills soaring through the roof: snow, ice, blizzards, blocked roads, closed airports and the 'good' news of a heating bill that has doubled!

The simple fact that this combination of adverse events may occur induced Enron's management to redefine the way the company was operated. The redefinition was predicated on the intuitive assumption that users of natural gas care mostly about reliable delivery and stable prices. Peter Tufano describes Enron's bold move as follows: 'Their vision was to create a "gas bank" that would serve as an intermediary between buyers and sellers, allowing both to shed their unwanted risks'. The move, although bold, was quite rational. Indeed, Enron's core asset is a deep knowledge of the natural gas market, from exploration to distribution. The new generation of Enron products was born. They were grouped together under a generic name 'EnFolio Gas Resource Agreements'. These agreements are customised according to the specific needs and requirements of customers. Thus, a customer can select a product called 'EnFolio GasCap', under which he receives a fixed quantity of gas at a price that varies according to a natural gas index but which can never rise above a specified ceiling. From being a producer and distributor of natural gas, Enron Capital and Trade Resources became a natural gas banker managing the volatility of the price of natural gas. This mutation has far-reaching implications. First, the methane molecule is no longer anonymous: it bears Enron's landmark. Second, to avoid failed promises, Enron had to make sure that it was properly equipped to monitor and trade the price risk of natural gas. To ensure this, it invested millions of dollars in the required technology and human capital. Nevertheless, the story would not have been a success if commodity derivatives had not been available. Enron would still be wondering how to redefine itself and the clients would still pray that prices remain stable. This molecule success story brings us to what Nobel Laureate and Stanford University Professor of Finance, William F. Sharpe, calls 'nuclear financial economics' (see Sharpe, 1995). Nuclear physicists investigate matter and the smallest particles that compose matter. Other things being equal, this is what 'nuclear financial economists' do. They investigate matter (read real economy and its myriad of risks), and try to 'virtually reshape' it by engineering and pricing proper instruments. Obviously, the more tradable the risks at their disposal, the more efficient their construction.

This type of risk management innovation is not the privilege of large corporations. Small businesses, too, can (and must) take advantage of it. Burns & McBride (Smithson and Smith, 1995) is a small family firm based in Wilmington, Delaware. It distributes heating oil to private households. Since 1990, its customers have been able to benefit from a fixed price for the whole winter. The sum of individual gas purchases provides Burns & McBride with the right critical mass to access the hedging markets. What each individual customer could not obtain on his own, Burns & McBride can, thanks simply to economies of scale. Despite the fact that it has to charge a slightly higher price for heating oil to cover the cost of insuring a guaranteed price, Burns & McBride has managed to increase the number of its customers.

Many other examples illustrate the same message. In Kentucky, a corporation called Paducah & Louisville Railroad (Smithson and Smith, 1995) transports coal, chemicals, stone and clay. Its locomotives consume about 500 000 gallons of fuel a month. Diesel fuel represents, on average, 10% of operating expenses. During an oil price crisis, this figure can double or even triple. In August 1990, Paducah & Louisville raised new equity to finance its growth. Investors were serene as they knew that Paducah & Louisville had properly hedged its diesel fuel exposure. Holiday-makers can also benefit from virtual finance. British tour operators offer holiday packages whose prices can be booked one year ahead despite, say, the fluctuations of the price of kerosene. For instance, Thomson, a tour operator and airline owner, has implemented kerosene hedging strategies and provided price guarantees for holidays booked one year in advance (Smithson and Smith, 1995). Very soon tour operators will also propose price rebates in the case of, say, lack of snow on a skiing holiday or sun on a beach holiday. No snow is no fun, especially if one paid a lot for the week. The rebate will not make snow, but it will ease the pain. The holiday-maker will pay only for what his or her vacation was really worth. This is possible only because derivatives are traded to cover weather risk. To paraphrase Enron's Nick Mooney, 'buy the weather you want for your holidays. The same opportunity applies to ski resorts that are heavily indebted to fund ski-tows, snow equipment and the like. The absence of snow may entail problems and the inability to face financial commitments. They, too, should consider alleviating the pain by 'buying the snow they want for their operations'.

Enrico Suppa and Baliano Grilli were really the farsighted fore-runners of the experts in modern finance, also known as 'rocket scientists'. Suppa, Grilli, Enron and others share a common characteristic: they are risk-tamers. Thanks to their efforts, mankind seems to know better than ever how to tame the risk Beast, how to come to terms with it. However, these modern victories over the gods, albeit fascinating, shall not be over-emphasised. History teaches us that the Beast has been hiding in the most unexpected places. Risk-tamers still have tremendous energy and imagination to deploy.

The lesson is clear. Nobel Laureate Robert C. Merton (1995) summarises it: 'Functions are always senior to institutions'. To put it more crudely, the client's needs are paramount. That said, the growing importance of virtual finance should not strike fear in our hearts. On the contrary, by shifting the focus of attention from institutions to functions, the virtual economy empowers market players to use their imagination to improve their products and services. Far from disrupting the real economy, then, virtual finance improves its vitality and creativity.

Modern global finance is cosmopolitan by nature. Cash flows do not carry passports. In a pamphlet (Bruckner, 1994), a French philosopher, Pascal Bruckner, wrote the following about cosmopolitanism: 'Moving from one civilization to another is like shedding one's skin, a metamorphosis which involves toil and work; a far cry from the smooth flight of the business jet that links all points on the planet'. According to Bruckner the cosmopolitans 'bring out something essential, upset opinions, bare the lie of closed societies'. Moving from one risk to another is, indeed, similar to shedding one's skin – a metamorphosis via the virtual economy. The fact that this metamorphosis can be achieved through instantaneous transactions does not mean that it is easy. Understanding and fighting the tyranny of the real economy requires wisdom, pugnacity and hard work.

This is something that is not always well understood, as is clearly demonstrated in recent essays. For instance, in 1995, the French sociologist Ignacio Ramonet (1996) coined the worrying notion of a 'PPII' system: planetary, permanent, immediate, immaterial. This system, according to Ramonet, is driven only by the 'easy and fast buck'. In this system, derivatives are viewed as some kind of evil, of permanent threat, as if they were living a life of their own. Ramonet, like many others, refuses to decipher the message. His stance reminds us of a famous Battle of Britain ace, the late Air Vice-Marshal John 'the Baron' Worrall. The Baron led a hurricane fighter squadron throughout the fall of France and the Battle of Britain. The story has it that in the middle of a fierce fight he held the following conversation with his controller (Massingberd, 1997):

Controller: '24 bombers with 20 plus more behind them.'
Worrall: 'Got it.'
Controller: '20 plus more bombers and 20 fighters behind and above.'
Worrall: 'All right.'
Controller: 'Now 30 more bombers and further 100 plus fighters following.'
Worrall: 'Stop. No more information please. You are frightening me terribly.'

Derivatives are in a sense very similar to Air Vice-Marshal Worrall's controller. They convey a message that some observers have decided either to read incorrectly or, worse, not to read at all.

   Yet, virtual finance is not cosmopolitan because the advent of the fax, computer, Internet and global networks has enabled a world-wide presence at the touch of a button. Virtual finance is cosmopolitan because it has to be if it wants to get a chance to circumvent or defeat the imperfections of the real economy. Risks cannot be shared at the single local level. They need more space. The nomadic nature of virtual finance is disliked, and even feared. As French economist, François Rachline (1991), pointed out, 'Today, the temptation is to assert that governments are no longer able to contain financial flows in both meanings of the word 'contain': block and monitor'. French sociologists Edgar Morin and Samir Nair (1999), note that by 'losing control of capital circulation society has lost control of the monster it has created', adding: 'Vast sums circulate daily without anyone knowing what they are for or which financial disaster they will cause'. These assertions are erroneous. The fluidity of modern finance is in sharp contrast to the viscidity of the real economy. It is deeply paradoxical that little is said about the viscidity of the real economy and how that penalises us all. Benedetto Zaccaria's talent and prowess turned out to be the stuff of legend, yet he may have taken them to his grave unnoticed had the physical world turned against him. That this was not the case, though, is as much to do with Baliano Grilli and Enrico Suppa as it had to do with the voyage to Bruges. They provided the outlet for Zaccaria's undeniable talents – for his good and the good of many who have since followed.

The harshness of the real economy is probably just as destructive as Charybdis, that ancient whirlpool in the Strait of Messina. That said, it is wrong to believe that, as an inevitable result of avoiding the real Charybdis, we will strike a virtual Scylla and sink without trace. Baliano Grilli and Enrico Suppa clearly knew a thing or two about seagoing dangers and they removed Benedetto Zaccaria's risks of pirates and storms nine centuries ago! Their task was undeniably difficult and it must be revisited and, indeed reinvented, time and again. It is reasonable to believe that, in this constant endeavour, virtual finance has a central role to play.

CONCLUSION

'Be of good heart: be of good spirit. If the battle is not yet won, it is not yet lost either'

Henry Hazlitt

Anyone who really wants to grasp economic matters must be wary of explanations that seem persuasive because they are both simple and obvious. Henry Hazlitt voiced the concern that 'the bad economists present their errors to the public better than good economists present their truths'. The same applies to financial matters. Finance does not get a good press. The fast growth of international financial markets is often viewed as a curse hanging over society. The Orange County abysmal losses, the October 1987 crash, and the Asian and Russian economic crises were waved in the press as disquieting signals. As Vanderbilt University Professor of Finance, Hans Stoll, and Duke University Professor of Finance, Robert Whaley, so rightly commented, the press often prefers to shoot the messenger rather than to take the time to decipher the message properly. This is what Henry Hazlitt meant when he criticised demagogues for presenting half-truths. Too often, the messenger is mistaken for the tyrant he tries to denounce. It is important not to pick the wrong target and blame an all-too-convenient scapegoat. Moreover, the detractors of financial markets do not seem to have anything to offer as an alternative. Henri Méchoulan (1990) asks a sensible question: 'In making money responsible for all evil, are we not doing liberty a disservice and are we not drawing attention away from other powers which might become established through the banning of all communication between people?"

These days, the name of the messenger is derivative products, virtual finance. He carries his news through computers. In the past, the messenger used telegram, cable or carrier pigeon! In this respect, it is quite amusing to note how short people's memories of financial affairs can be. For example, October 1987 was immediately compared to October 1929. But, those who blamed the virtual economy for triggering the 1987 crash would have been well advised to study economic history more carefully. What was said in France at the time of the financial crash that occurred in Lyon in January 1882 is quite interesting:

The reason for the repercussions of the crash being greater in Lyon than Paris is to be found in certain local characteristics of the behaviour of banking and share-trading circles in the Lyon marketplace, where speculation was practised to an excessive degree. The crash nevertheless affected all the financial marketplaces, in the provinces and in Paris. Share prices fluctuated more or less simultaneously and the use of telegrams was largely responsible for this. (Bouvier, 1974)

Certainly, commentators at the time had plenty of excuses for not fully understanding the situation. They did not benefit from the high-performance tools which modern economic analysis provides. Far fewer specialised publications were available. Any critical examination of a financial crisis was therefore bound to be superficial, and full of hypotheses that generally were impossible to verify.

Since those days the situation has changed greatly and today it seems inconceivable that anyone could undertake a critical analysis of economic and financial events without the valuable stock of knowledge made available by economics and financial theory. Unfortunately, this knowledge, even when applied with great rigour, is not always sufficient and there are still some grey areas to be clarified by economic and financial research. Nevertheless, sound ideas and concepts have become firmly established.

First, the thinking process followed by the critics of financial markets is flawed. These critics rise up against the intolerable costs that society has to bear because of the so-called primacy of the financial markets. But what are they suggesting as an alternative? And, if they do, in fact, have any solutions to offer, should one naively believe that these solutions will entail no cost at all for anyone? More to the point, have they shown that the costs of their counter-proposals is markedly lower than those which they ascribe to the dreaded financial markets? As always in economics, costs have to be looked at on a marginal basis. And, it is fair to say that, so far, critics of financial markets have failed to provide us with a thorough analysis that weighs the marginal benefits and the marginal costs of their economic recipes.

Second, it cannot be denied that financial markets, and especially derivatives, enable economic agents to achieve a better balance between profitability and risk that would be difficult to achieve otherwise. And, as Yale University's Robert Shiller has shown, current derivatives markets are doing a small portion of the job. Significant risks are still not traded, hence not shared. Hence, the cost of banning derivatives is pretty clear: a slower economic growth.

Third, it is often said that financial markets destroy industrial initiative, that they distract the entrepreneur from his real business. French economist François Chesnais (1996) rebels against this 'financialisation' of industrial groups. In his view, the time horizon within which a company's investments have to yield a return is considerably reduced under the dictatorship of the financial markets. According to him, the permanent pressure exerted by the financial leviathan has a harmful effect on investment, employment and industrial research. Short-term profitability has become the only parameter acknowledged by the markets. CEOs sacrifice long-term considerations in order to ensure that their quarterly results please the financial analysts' community. This is a rather surprising perspective, quite apart from the fact that it contradicts all the authoritative studies on the subject (see Woolridge, 1988). Indeed, this short-termism argument is easily debunked by looking at the US equity market – considered by many people as the most myopic of all. Recent studies of the 30 companies that make up the Dow-Jones index show that 80%–90% of the value of these companies is attributable to expected dividends beyond a five-year horizon. In other words, the price at which 'professional creditors' buy and sell shares in industrial companies is based on a long-term view. The market is neither short-sighted nor long-sighted: it has 20/20 vision. It is not even necessary to refer to the famous theorems coined by MIT Nobel Laureate, Franco Modigliani, and University of Chicago Nobel Laureate, Merton H. Miller[1] to be convinced that finance, however

---

[1] According to these two authors, in a perfect world (with no taxes, no bankruptcy costs, perfect information), the choice of how to finance a business (i.e. the mix of equity and debt) has no impact on the value of the business. More prosaically, that amounts to saying that the size of a cake is not affected by the way in which it is sliced.

modern or virtual it may be, means nothing unless it is underpinned by intense economic activity. In his *Eloge de Monsieur de Gournay*, Anne Robert Jacques Turgot (see Laurent, 1997), a minister under Louis XVI, reminded those who had forgotten that 'finance therefore must not be allowed to harm commerce, since this would be harmful to itself'.

To put it in a nutshell, finance fulfils three main functions: it evaluates (in other words, measures the size of the cake), distributes (cuts the cake) and transfers risks. Finance, contrary to a view held by many, is not a means of creating wealth out of nothing, except, of course, where arbitrage opportunities are available.[2] Its mandate is to quantify the wealth produced by the economy and to allocate it among the various economic agents by means of suitable assets or portfolio strategies. At the same time, risk engineers design hedging tools to immunise this wealth against unexpected risk occurrences. Financial innovation is of no purpose if it does not address wealth allocation or risk issues. To take the particular case of fluctuations in the price of tuna, the aim is not to eliminate price volatility by some kind of virtual magic. It is rather to ensure that the risk is better shared among the various stakeholders.

Finally, it might be useful to recall once again the crucial role played by reliable information, rapidly transmitted. The financial marketplace is particularly experienced in the art of decoding, interpreting and transmitting information. Arbitrage, computers and

---

[2] Arbitrage is not a complicated operation. For example, two markets for identical candies ought to be quoted the same price. But, if they are not, then buy the cheap one and sell it on the 'expensive' market. As a result, the law of one price for identical commodities will prevail.

derivatives are among the tools which ensure that information is efficiently circulated. The twentieth-century manager is without a doubt better off than the fifteenth-century merchant. In French historian Jean Favier's words:

The communication of news was less easy. Whether in written or verbal form, news was generally carried in the same way. A traveller would willingly undertake to deliver some letters, although it might mean not handing them over to the recipients until after he had seen to his own affairs and taken the time to pass on the most important items of news to his own family – sometimes he would be quite open and honest about his intention of doing this. Anyone depending on someone else's courier would inevitably be served last. But not everyone could afford a courier; the cost of sending messages put couriers beyond the reach of almost anyone but wealthy aristocrats.... The messenger sometimes never got past the first patch of woodland. (Favier, 1987)

So should one be complaining today about the fact that one has easy access to messengers and that these messengers no longer fear 'the dangers of the forest'? Should one regret the passing of the glorious era of the Antwerp pigeon, a highly prized breed of homing pigeon renowned for its dense plumage and its ability to fly in strong winds and which, even if it managed to escape all the dangers on its journey, unfortunately could only carry its messages and news between May and September? Of course not! The fact is, just as the barometer fall predicts but does not cause rain, the 'virtual' financial markets fill an essential role as 'financial weather' forecasters.

To close this book, we should like to make the final point that finance is to today's citizen what geography was to the businessman in the Middle Ages. 'Many businessmen were aware of what they gained from having accurate information about the world. Knowledge of geography was already regarded as necessary for the formation of economic policy. Resources, customers, distances, local customs, everything could one day become the basis of either wise choices or costly errors' (Favier, 1987).

Finance has undoubtedly never been so much in the minds of all economic decision-makers as it is today. This is not at all surprising. The more finance becomes virtual, the more it becomes part of the reality of our daily life. A mere 10 years ago, financial research was confined to a small circle of the initiated, and this exclusiveness was held against it. Today, all that has changed. Modern financiers, the 'cyber-financiers', actively participate in the bold innovations of economic decision-makers and entrepreneurs, and contribute to their success. We hope this book has provided convincing evidence that their contribution is a valuable one.

REFERENCES

Aesop, (1906) *Fables*, London: Everyman's Library.

Athanasoulis, S., Schiller, R. and van Wincoop, E. (1999) Macro markets and financial security, *Federal Reserve Bank of New York Economic Policy Review*, April.

Bainville, J. (1937) *La Fortune de la France*, Paris: Librairie Plon.

Barnes, J. (1995) *Letters from London, 1990–1995*, London: Vintage Books.

Barro, R.J. (1999) My luncheon with Bono, Economic Viewpoint, *Business Week* 7 December.

Bastiat, F. (1850) *Ce qu'on voit et ce qu'on ne voit pas, Choix de Sophismes et de Pamphlets Economiques*, reprinted 1993, Paris: Romillat. See also the English version on the website: www.freedomsnest.com/bastiat.html.

Bernstein, P. (1993) *Capital Ideas*, New York: Free Press.

Bono (2000) Le Plus Beau des Harcèlements, *Le Monde*, 7 January, p 14.

Bourdieu, P. (1994) *Raisons Pratiques. Sur la Théorie de l'Action*, Paris: Seuil. English translation: *Practical Reasons. On the Theory of Action* (1998) Stanford: Stanford University Press.

Bourguinat, H. (1995) *La tyrannie des marchés, Essai sur l'économie virtuelle*, Paris: *Economica*.

Bouvier, J. (1974) Les crises économiques, in *Faire de l'Histoire*, Folio, Paris: Gallimard.

Braudel, F. (1979) *Civilisation Matérielle, Économie et Capitalisme*, Paris: Le Livre de Poche. English translation: *Civilization and Capitalism: 15th–18th Century* (1992) Los Angeles: The University of California Press.

Bronk, R. (1999) *Progress and the Invisible Hand. The Philosophy and Economics of Human Advance*, New York: Warner Books.

Bruckner, P. (1994) *Le Vertige de Babel, Cosmopolitisme et Mondialisme*, Paris: Arléa.

Chesnais, F. (1996) Mondialisation du capital et régime d'accumulation à dominante financière, *Agone*, No.16, pp. 15–39.

Chesneaux, J. (1996) *Habiter le Temps*, Paris: Société, Bayard Editions.

Cohen, D. (1994) *Les Infortunes de la Prospérité*, Paris: Julliard. English translation: *The Misfortunes of Prosperity: An Introduction to Modern Political Economy* (1995) Boston: MIT Press.

Dacunha-Castelle, D. (1996) *Chemins de l'Aléatoire*, Paris: Flammarion.

de la Vega, J. (1688) *Confusión de Confusiones*, Boston: Baker Library, Harvard Graduate School of Business Administration.

Dickens, C. (1843) *A Christmas Carol*, new edition 1997, New York: Holt, Rinehart and Winston.

Dunbar, N. (1999) *Inventing Money*, London: John Wiley & Sons.

Edelstein, R. and Paul, J.-M. (1998) Europe needs a new financial paradigm, *The Wall Street Journal Europe*, 12–13 June.

Edwards, F.R. (1996) *The New Finance, Regulation and Financial Stability*, Washington DC: The AEI Press.

Favier, J. (1987) *De l'Or et des Épices, Naissance de l'Homme d'Affaires au Moyen Age*, Paris: Fayard. English translation: *Gold and Spices: The Rise of Commerce in the Middle Ages* (1998) New York: Holmes & Meier Publishers.

Favier, J. (1991) *Les Grandes Découvertes*, Paris: Le Livre de Poche.

Friedman, M. (1988) Why the twin deficits are a blessing, *The Wall Street Journal*, 14 December.

Geronimo (1970) *Geronimo. His Own Story*, New York: E.P. Dutton. See also www.//odur.let.rug.nl/~usa/B/geronimo/geronixx.1

Giddens, A. (1999) *Runaway World: How Globalisation is Reshaping our Lives*, London: Profile Books.

Gray, J. (1999) *False Dawn. The Delusions of Global Capitalism*, London: Granta Books.

Gustin, P. (1996) L'assurance, fille du commerce et de la mer, *Enjeux Les Echos*, July–August, p. 88.

Hazlitt, H. (1946) *Economics in One Lesson*, New York: Harper & Brothers, re-published by Crown Publishers (1979) New York. See also the following websites: www.hazlitt.org, www.laissezfaire.org/

Henwood, D. (1998) *Wall Street. How it Works and for Whom*, New York: Verso.

Krugman, P. (1994) The myth of Asia's miracle, *Foreign Affairs*, November–December, 62–78.

Laurent, A. ed. (1997) Turgot, Laissez Faire!, Paris: *Les Belles Lettres*.

Le Goff, J. (1986) *La Bourse et la Vie. Textes du XXe Siècle*, Paris: Hachette.

Lewis, M. (1989) *Liar's Poker*, London: Hodder and Stoughton.

Londres, A. (1929) *Terre d'Ébène, La Traite des Noirs*, 2nd edn 1994, Paris: Le Serpent à Plumes.

Londres, A. (1931) *Pêcheurs de Perles*, 2nd edn 1994, Paris: Le Serpent à Plumes.

Mandel, M.J. (1996) *The High-risk Society. Peril and Promise in the New Economy*, New York: Random House.

Massingberd, H. ed. (1997) *The Daily Telegraph Second Book of Obituaries*, London: Pan Books.

Méchoulan, H. (1990) *Amsterdam au Temps de Spinoza*, Paris: Argent et Liberté.

Merton, R.C. et al. (1995) *The Global Financial System: A Functional Perspective*, Boston: Harvard Business School Press.

Miller, M.H. (1997) *Merton Miller on Derivatives*, New York: John Wiley & Sons.

Montesquieu, C. de (1721) *Lettres Persones*, reprinted 1992, Classiques Garnier, Paris: Bordas.

Morand, P. (1937) *Eloge du Repos*, Paris: Flammarion. New edition published by Arléa, 1996.

Morin, E. and Naïr, S. (1999) *Une Politique de Civilisation*, Paris: Arléa.

Newberry, D.M. (1989) Futures markets, hedging and speculation, in John Eatwell, Murray Milgate and Peter Newman (eds) *Finance, The New Palgrave*, London and Basingstoke: Macmillan Reference Books.

Olson, M. (1982) *The rise and decline of Nations, Economic Growth, Stagflation and Social Rigidities*, New Haven, CT: Yale University Press.

Ortner, R. (1990) *Voodoo Deficits*, Homewood, Ill.: Dow Jones–Irwin.

Price, D.E. (1959) Is man becoming obsolete? US Public Health Reports, **74**, (8).

Rachline, F. (1991) *De Zéro à Epsilon, vers une Nouvelle Théorie de l'Économie*, Paris: FIRST.

Rambaud, J. (1895) *Eléments d'Economie Politique*, Lyon: Auguste Cote.

Ramonet, I. (1996) *Nouveaux Pouvoirs, Nouveaux Maîtres du Monde*, Montreal: Editions Fides.

Say, J.-B. (1821) *Cours d'Économie Politique et Autres Essais*, reprinted 1996, Paris: Flammarion. English translation: *An Economist in Troubled Times: Writings* (1997) Princeton: Princeton University Press.

Sharpe, W.F. (1995) Nuclear financial economics, in William H. Beaver and George Parker (eds) *Risk Management, Problems and Solutions*, Stanford University, Financial Services Research Initiative, New York: McGraw Hill.

Shiller, R.J. (1998) *Macro Markets. Creating Institutions for Managing Society's Largest Economic Risks*, Clarendon Lecture in Economics, Oxford: Oxford University Press.

Smith, A. (1776) An inquiry into the nature of the wealth of nations, reprinted in R.H. Campbell and A.S. Skinner (eds) *The Glasgow Edition of the Works and Correspondence of Adam Smith* (1979) Oxford: Clarendon Press.

Smithson, C.W. and Smith, C.W. Jr, (1995) *Managing Financial Risk*, New York: Richard D. Irwin Inc.,

Stevenson, R.L. (1878) *Materials of Travels with a Donkey*, manuscript HM 2408, Huntington Library, San Marino, California.

Strange, S. (1997) *Casino Capitalism*, Manchester: Manchester University Press.

Stulz, R.M. (1996) Rethinking risk management, the quarterly interview, *CEMS Business Review*, **1**, (3).

The Economist (1999) Millenium special edition, 1 January 1000–31 December 1999, pp. 97–98.

Thrapp, D.L. (1964) *The Conquest of Apacheria*, Norman: University of Oklahoma Press.

Tufano, P. (1996) How financial engineering can advance corporate strategy, *Harvard Business Review*, January–February.

Verne, J. (1873) *Around the World in Eighty Days*, Paris: J. Hetzel et Cie; reprinted Penguin Classics, 1999.

Warde, I. (1995) La tyrannie de l'economiquement correct, *Le Monde Diplomatique*, May, 20–21.

White, L. (1991) *The S & L Debacle*, Oxford: Oxford University Press.

Woolridge, R. (1988) Competitive decline and corporate restructuring: is a myopic stock market to blame?, in *Continental Bank Journal of Applied Corporate Finance*, Spring, pp. 26–36.

Wright, K.M. (1991) The structure, conduct and regulation of the life insurance industry, in R.W. Kopcke and R.E. Randall (eds), *The Financial Condition and Regulation of Insurance Companies* (1991) Boston: Federal Reserve Bank of Boston.

Ymbert, J.-G. (1825) *L'Art de faire des Dettes par un Homme comme il faut*. New edition published by Rivages Poche, Paris, 1996.

Young, A. (1992) A tale of two cities: factor accumulation and technical change in Hong Kong and Singapore, *NBER Macroeconomics Annual*, Cambridge, MA: The MIT Press.

Young, A. (1994) The tyranny of numbers: confronting the statistical realities of the East Asian growth experience, NBER Working Paper No. 4680, March.

Zola, E. (1911) *L'Argent*, London: Schoenhofs Foreign Books. English translation: *Money* (1991) Pocket Classics series, London: Sutton Publishing.